THE SEVEN HILLS
OF
ABERGAVENNY

by
Chris Barber

[signature: Chris Barber]

Blorenge Books
Abergavenny, Gwent
1992

[inscription: John Hayward 4/1996.]

First Published 1992

ISBN 1 872730 02 7

© Chris Barber

BLORENGE
BOOKS

3, Holywell Road, Abergavenny, Gwent NP7 5LP.
Tel: Abergavenny 853909.

Text output by Able Typesetters, Unit 27, Enterprise Way,
Newport, Gwent NP9 2AQ. Tel: (0633) 244534.

Printed by Mid Wales Litho Ltd., Units 12/13, Pontyfelin Avenue,
Pontypool, Gwent.

In memory of my father Bill Barber
who introduced me to Skirrid Fawr
and the pleasures of wandering
the hills with a camera

Skirrid Fawr (The Holy Mountain). *Chris Barber*

CONTENTS

Introduction
Guidelines for Walkers
The Seven Hills of Abergavenny
Route 1 Walking the Seven Hills

BLORENGE
Route 2 Around the Summit Plateau
Route 3 Up the Incline
Route 4 Hill's Tramroad
Route 5 Ascent from Govilon

MYNYDD PEN Y FAL (Sugar Loaf)
Route 6 The Easy Way
Route 7 Through St. Mary's Vale
Route 8 The Back Door Route
Route 9 Llwyn Du Circuit
Route 10 Glangrwyne Circuit

ABERGAVENNY — 'The Gateway to Wales'
Route 11 The Massacre Walk
Route 12 Llanwenarth Church
Route 13 Ascent of the Graig
Route 14 Odd Corners of Abergavenny
Route 15 Up the River and down the Canal

SKIRRID FAWR — 'The Holy Mountain'
Route 16 The Traditional Way
Route 17 The Hard Way

ADDITIONAL INFORMATION
The Three Peaks Trial
Local Facilities
Nine Hundred Years in the History of Abergavenny

INTRODUCTION

This little book is the result of my wanderings around the Abergavenny area over many years. I have found it very satisfying to study and explore my doorstep in such detail for it is possible to accomplish a great deal without making much use of a vehicle. To live in or near Abergavenny is particularly rewarding if you are a keen and active walker, for just like Rome it is said to be cradled by seven hills. They are not only good to look at but also provide excellent scope for stretching the legs and enjoying views in all directions. Many people who buy this book will perhaps be curious to find out the names of these seven hills. Four of them can be guessed quite easily, but the remaining three do not come to mind so readily. All will be revealed in due course!

People who have lived in Abergavenny all their lives often remark to me 'Yes, I've been up the Sugar Loaf, but only once, and that was about twenty years ago.' They obviously are not true walkers and to them the ascent of the Sugar Loaf is just something that only needs to be achieved once in order to be able to say that they have been to its summit. Having accomplished that they have been content merely to gaze upwards at the Blorenge and Skirrid Fawr, the two other dominant peaks overlooking their town.

To know these hills intimately you need to ascend to their summits on numerous occasions and at varying times of the year. It is ony then that you can appreciate their moods and the ever-changing views, across the Vale of Usk, to the Black Mountains and eastern Gwent. Also you need to explore all the established routes to these summits and seek out the lesser known ways as well.

It is necessary to struggle up the steep inclines on the brooding Blorenge and explore the tramroads and tunnels, where the sheep now wander and visitors pause to ponder on the origin and purpose of yesterday's endeavours and dreams; seek out the hollow known as the Punch-bowl and imagine the mountain men prize fighting a hundred years ago in this secret place.

Walk through St. Mary's Vale in the autumn and revel in the startling colours. Climb Skirrid Fawr in early spring and see the snowdrops and primroses in the woods clothing the lower slopes of this fascinating hill. Stand on the summit of Sugar Loaf in the darkness and look down on the twinkling lights of Abergavenny and it will seem as if you have never been there before. Come here on a clammy grey November day or in a keen March wind that cuts like a razor and you will not linger on the summit, but pause briefly to touch the trig' point and then descend to escape from nature's cold and buffeting force.

On another occasion you may struggle to your chosen summit through driving rain, strong wind, stinging hail-stones or perhaps the flurry of a blizzard to reach an ice-encrusted trig' point. On such occasions, the times when you sweated your way upwards on a hot summer afternoon will seem unreal and hard to imagine. But to experience such a wide variety of weather conditions will enrich your knowledge and appreciation of these hills so that every ascent becomes a memorable one.

A mist-enveloped hill is an emotional one for it can conjour up feelings of sadness and solemnity emphasising the possibility that no-one but you or your party are out walking that day. Even rain has its attractions for on some days it will ensure wonderful clarity to the views when a gap appears in the clouds and shafts of sunlight suddenly make it all seem so worthwhile.

Snow can also provide a touch of magic even though it glares in the sun, makes your legs ache when it is deep and your feet wet when it gets into your boots. But you will always long to see it on the hills again and take delight in plodding your way through a fairy land that bears no resemblance to the route that you are normally used to following.

Different companions will also make your walk more interesting, or depending on their degree of enthusiasm, perhaps less enjoyable. Alternatively you may prefer to walk alone, for as a solitary walker you can benefit physically from the exercise while all your problems pale into insignificance, now that you are once again walking your favourite hill blowing the cobwebs away.

When introducing friends to your local paradise it is always useful to know a few local legends and tales, and be familiar with local landmarks and items of interest that can be pointed out during the chosen walk. This area has a wealth of fascinating history and legends, dating from prehistoric times to the present day. In this book I have tried to include a wide selection of such information and also to tell the history of Abergavenny itself. From Roman times to the present day the stories are intriguing and include accounts of Norman lords, native Welsh princes, pioneers of industry and local characters. The important thing is that they were all people who have helped to shape the history of this very special locality and have left their mark on the landscape.

So I will look forward to seeing you on the 'Seven Hills of Abergavenny' and I hope that these routes will give you as much pleasure over the coming years as I have experienced since I first became drawn to their fascinating slopes and summits.

Chris Barber
Llanfoist
1992

Looking towards the summit of Sugar Loaf.   *Chris Barber*

GUIDELINES FOR WALKERS

'My favourite mountain is the one that I happen to be on at the time.'
                                                    Alfred Wainwright

The following reminders will generally be familiar to most readers but they are offered as a guide to walkers of limited experience.

EQUIPMENT
Take warm and waterproof clothes when venturing on the hills and wear sensible footwear. Waterproofs should always be carried as a matter of habit. In winter take additional items such as gloves, hat and extra sweater. In exceptional conditions when the summits are encrusted with ice or hard snow, an ice axe may even be desirable. Always carry a map, compass, torch and first aid kit as part of your standard equipment.

MAPS
Ordnance Survey 1: 25,000 (2½ inches), Outdoor Leisure Map of the Brecon Beacons National Park (Eastern Area) or Pathfinder Sheet SO 21/31.

WEATHER
Obtain a local weather forecast before setting out for the hills. The local Weathercall number is 0898 500414.

TIMING

The times given for the routes in this book are only a general guide. It is very difficult to give precise timings as so many variable factors have to be taken into account. You are advised to plan your walks with a generous time allowance and be prepared to turn back or change your route if the weather deteriorates.

ROUTE FINDING

If you intend to lead a party around an unfamiliar walk, always check the route out beforehand so that you can be sure of finding the right way. Your followers will be particularly impressed with the quality of your leadership if you appear to know the route so well that you hardly bother to use the map.

ACCIDENTS

In the event of an accident seek the nearest telephone. Dial 999 and state the nature of injuries and location. If possible arrange for one of the party to stay by the 'phone until help arrives.

INTERNATIONAL DISTRESS SIGNAL

Six blasts of the whistle, shouts or flashes of a torch — followed by a minute silence and then repeated. Never blow a whistle or flash a torch uneccessarily.

PLEASE REMEMBER AND RESPECT THE COUNTRY CODE

Enjoy the countryside and respect its life and work.
Guard against the risk of all fire.
Fasten all gates.
Keep your dog under control.
Keep to public footpaths across farmland.
Use gates and stiles to cross fences, hedges and walls.
Leave livestock, crops and machinery alone.
Take your litter home.
Help to keep all water clean.
Protect wildlife, plants and trees.
Take special care on country roads.
Make no unnecessary noise.

THE SEVEN HILLS OF ABERGAVENNY

Abergavenny, the ancient Roman fortress of Gobannium, has something in common with Rome, for both locations are surrounded by seven hills. A tight loop of the Tiber half encircles Rome while Abergavenny sits beside the Rivers Usk and Fenni. Four dominant peaks and three distinctive rounded humps overlook the town providing an impression that it is situated in the centre of a great ampitheatre.

Many visitors who come here are fascinated by these shapely hills and keen walkers find the challenge of their ascent irresistible. During the last two decades an event known as The Three Peaks Trial has become well established as an annual endurance walk involving the ascent of the Blorenge, Sugar Loaf and Skirrid Fawr in an 18 mile walk. However this popular event was preceded by one that offered an even greater challenge and it became known as the Seven Hills Race, now largely forgotten.

A record was set up for running over the Seven Hills of Abergavenny by Percy Fraser (Junior) and Paddy Sherman who first went round the route in 6 hours 6 minutes. However they both felt that they could improve considerably on this time and on 27th March 1949 they had another go and reduced it dramatically to 4 hours 54 minutes.

On April 10th 1954 an open Mountain Marathon Race was held at Abergavenny over the Seven Hills route. It was organised by Mr. Les Williams, a local long distance runner. Changing rooms were to have been at the Vine Tree Inn, St. John's Square, but this arrangement was altered and the National Fire Service Hut was used instead. There were eleven competitors and the race was started from the Town Hall by the Mayor of Abergavenny, Councillor J.A. Morgan who also presented the prizes at the end.

Only five of the field of eleven managed to finish the course and as the remaining runners began the ascent of Skirrid Fach, F.C. Bailey of Preston looked like being the winner, but Les Williams a 48 years old Newport Harriers Runner from Gilwern managed to overhaul him and reached the Town Hall in the excellent time of 4 hours 10 minutes and 22 seconds. Second place went to M.T. Withrell of Preston, in 4hours 19 minutes and 9 seconds. F.C. Badley took third place in 4 hours 22 minutes 46 seconds.

Five years later Ken Flowers and Ray Hardee, two Abergavenny cross-country runners decided to attempt to establish a new record on April 17th, 1959. Choosing April was probably a mistake for it is traditionally a rather wet month. In fact heavy overnight and early morning rain made the route a sea of mud. Ray unfortunately developed cramp half way round the course and Ken had to massage his legs to get him going again. They were then chased by barking dogs as they passed through a farmyard and the wet conditions certainly slowed them up in several places. The marshall on the summit of Skirrid Fawr later commented, 'I had taken my time getting up to the top and was looking for a sheltered spot when, to my amazement, I saw them climbing at a steady pace. They were an hour ahead of the previous time. After a brief pause for

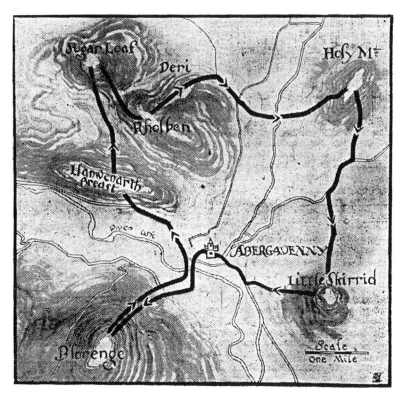

Route of the 'Seven Hills' Record Run.

Employees from British Nylon Spinners acted as time keepers and marshalls on the course and the times recorded were:-

Start from Town Hall at	*10.00a.m.*
Blorenge Summit	*10.35*
Llanwenarth Breast	*11.22*
Sugar Loaf Summit	*11.42*
Rholben	*11.51*
Skirrid Fawr	*12.35*
Skirrid Fach	*1.48*
Town Hall	*2.04*

Ken Flowers and Ray Hardee setting off from the Town Hall.

Descending the 'Big Drop' on the Blorenge incline.

some coffee and a tot of rum, they then ran off on the last lap'. In due course they arrived back at the Town Hall, mud-spattered, tired and triumphant, for they brought the record down to an impressive 4 hours 4 minutes and 5 seconds, breaking the previous best time by just under 50 minutes. At the finish they were congratulated by Mr. H. G. Husbands, President of the Abergavenny Chamber of Trade.

When interviewed by 'The Abergavenny Chronicle' Ken Flowers told the reporter that he was confident that the run could be done in an even faster time. He felt that he could shorten it by at least half an hour. However he would wait for other runners to have a go at beating the record and then have another crack at it himself.

An attempt was made on the new record by a Grammar School student and a friend of his from St. Luke's College, Exeter. Alan Ponter and Keith Brigstock returned the time of 7 hours 40 minutes. Afterwards they both commented that they should have taken more care in planning their route.

Eleven years later Ken Flowers and Peter Maloney decided to have a go at reducing the record even further. For six months before their attempt they were in strict training and carried out several practice runs over the route. Councillor John Lewis set them off and by the time they had reached the fifth summit they were 19 minutes ahead of Ken's previous time. They then slowed up for a while and their advantage dropped to eight minutes, but they made it up on the homeward stretch. They triumphantly arrived back at the Town Hall having successfully reduced the Seven Hills record to 3 hours 24 minutes and 46 seconds, smashing the previous time by 39 minutes 19 seconds.

Afterwards, Ken Flowers said, 'I could not have wished for a better running partner than Peter Maloney. We both inspired each other. Peter is keen to have another go at the route but, at 38, I think that this will have to be my last attempt. I am very pleased with the new record but it would give me great pleasure to see other runners having a crack at it'.

Len Evans, who was a marshall on the summit of the Blorenge, brought along his dog, Bob, a mixture of old English sheepdog and terrier. When Sherman and Fraser had set up the record ten years previously, Bob was just six months old, and actually followed the runners over the whole course. 'He loves the hills', said Len, 'and I believe he would have repeated his feat had I let him'.

ROUTE 1

WALKING THE SEVEN HILLS (26 miles, allow 9-10 hours)

This is a very energetic walk and the complete route in one day should only be undertaken if you are feeling particularly fit. It is not advisable to attempt it on a hot day. Some people may prefer to do it over two days with a descent to Abergavenny from the Deri ridge providing a good end to the first day.

When the Seven Hills record was established the route chosen would not have been based on Rights of Way for the runners would have taken the shortest possible distance between the seven check points to save as much time as possible. The following route is one that I have devised for walkers and it is entirely on rights of way. It also involves walking the full lengths of the Llanwenarth, Rholben and Deri spurs instead of merely 'bagging' the highest points on those ridges.

The traditional starting point has always been the Town Hall, so park at one of the many car parks in Abergavenny and make your way to the clock tower to start this challenging walk.

Make your way to Castle Meadows and then over Llanfoist Bridge. Cross the road with care at the end of the bridge and follow the lane past the cemetery. In due course it passes beneath the Heads of the Valleys Road and leads to the B4246.

Cross the road and continue up Church Lane, passing Llanfoist Church on the left. At the top of the lane go through the tunnel under the canal and then cross a stile directly opposite the tunnel mouth.

Continue beside a stream and up through the woods following a steep incline. Go past a small brick building and shortly cross a stile. At the top of the next stage of the incline you will emerge from the trees. Cross a field and make for the stile directly above.

Pause to catch your breath and admire the view which is now opening up to include the Sugar Loaf, Skirrid Fawr and Skirrid Fach and the ever growing sprawl of Abergavenny.

From the stile continue upwards with a fence on your right. When the fence bends to the right, head straight on following a path directly up the north face of the Blorenge. It is a steep ascent but certainly not as daunting as it looks from Llanfoist village.

On gaining the top of the escarpment, a new view opens up to the south across the Bristol Channel. Walk on past the small red brick building and follow a well trodden path up the gently rising ground. The large cairn and trig' point on the summit of the Blorenge will soon be seen (559 metres).

From the summit head in a north westerly direction on a bearing of 284 degrees.

Thread your way through the heather, bracken and boulders enjoying a new view of the Vale of Usk, Brecon Beacons and Black Mountains. On reaching a tramroad you need to find the path junction at SO 265119.

Follow this path down through the bracken. It provides an easy-angled des-

14

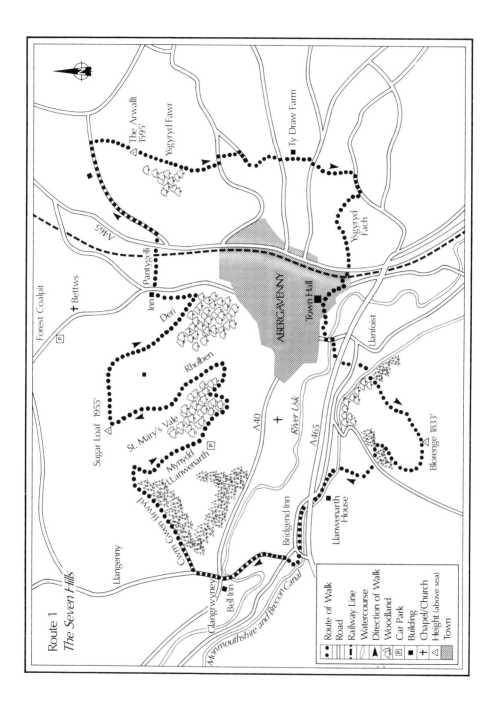

Route 1
The Seven Hills

The Arwallt 1595'
Ysgyryd Fawr
Ty Draw Farm
Ysgyryd Fach
A465
Pantygelli
Inn
Bettws
Forest Coalpit
Deri
ABERGAVENNY
Town Hall
Llanfoist
Rholben
Sugar Loaf 1955'
St. Mary's Vale
A40
River Usk
A465
Blorenge 1833'
Mynydd
Llanwenarth
Llangenny
Cwm Gwyn llwyd
Bridgend Inn
Llanwenarth House
Clangrwyney
Bell Inn
Monmouthshire and Brecon Canal

•:•		Route of Walk
|||		Road
! ! !		Railway Line
		Watercourse
▲		Direction of Walk
🌲		Woodland
P		Car Park
■		Building
+		Chapel/Church
△		Height (above sea)
▦		Town

15

cent and is particularly useful when the bracken is chest-high. Join Hill's Tramroad by a well preserved set of holed stones that once supported the tram rails and follow it to the right. Look out for a stone wall on the left and then go down to a stile. From here a path is waymarked down through the trees. It is a pleasant track carpeted with pine needles and flanked by moss covered stone walls.

Emerge from the wood, go over a stile and, cross the road. On the opposite side, go down a steep path which soon snakes around the hillside and provides views across to the Sugar Loaf. Pass through a small wooden gate and keep left along the path which soon becomes a stony track and leads down to a road. Turn right.

Keep straight on at the next road junction and pass the 'Old School House' on the left. Turn left at the next junction, cross a stone bridge over an old railway line, then go left and shortly cross a stile on the right. Follow a path down beside a fence and the cross a field to reach a wooden footbridge spanning a chuckling stream. Turn right beside the stream and then follow the path beside a fence with the canal now appearing on your right. Notice the metal boundary marker posts.

Cross a stile and descend some steps to reach a road. Turn right and pass beneath the canal and then immediately turn right up some stone steps which lead up to the canal towpath. Follow the towpath to the right.

As you pass Bridge 100 you will see Llanwenarth House on the left. This ancient house used to be the home of Sir Morgan Llwyd (in English — 'Lloyd') who had the present house built in 1539. He was rector of the parish and claimed paternal descent from Sitsyllt ap Dyfnawl, who was murdered by William de Braose at the notorious massacre in Abergavenny Castle in 1177.

Pass beneath the Heads of the Valleys Road and leave the canal at the Bridgend Inn. Cross the road and go down the lane beside the Canal Craft Shop. After about 20 yards descend some steps on the left and follow a path down into a dingle where the River Clydach roars beneath a stone bridge. Turn left and follow the road past Dan y Bont Mill. On reaching the main road turn left along a pavement and just past the garage cross the road and turn right beside the Corn Exchange. Follow this road to reach a metal bridge over the Usk. It squeaks and rattles as you walk over it.

Continue up to the Bell Inn and then turn right along the pavement. Shortly cross the A40 and turn up the lane leading to Llangenny. Take the first turning on the right and follow this road up for nearly a mile to reach the point where it comes to an end. Cross a stile on the right and turn left beside a fence to follow a broad cart track past a derelict barn. The summit of the Sugar Loaf can be seen looming in the distance.

After about ½ mile, the track descends towards the dingle of Cwm Gwenffrwd. Follow the narrow path gently ascending the bank on the left. It leads up to a gate. From here continue along the stony path overlooking the dingle with the Afon Gwenffrwd chattering past below.

Follow the path around the edge of a field, go through a small gate and walk across the next field. The path now descends to another gate. From here it bends around the side of the valley and drops down to a stream crossing. Go up the steep slope on the other side. At the top of the slope, go straight across a junction of tracks. The summit of the Sugar Loaf now seems tantalisingly close but our route now lies down the Llanwenarth spur.

At the next track junction turn right and shortly go straight on at the following set of tracks, to make your way down the crest of the Llanwenarth ridge. The summits of Sugar Loaf, Skirrid Fawr, Skirrid Fach and Blorenge are now all visible, reminding you of your purpose.

Near the end of the ridge bear left past an area of grassy hollows, where building stone was once quarried and then follow the track around to the right to meet a road. Turn left down the road which sadly descends for some distance, losing much precious height. Keep straight on at the next road junction and then almost immediately bear left along a cart track.

Llanwenarth Breast and the Sugar Loaf.   *Chris Barber*

Look out for a stile on the right which you cross and then go steeply down beside a fence to reach another stile. Now head down bearing slightly right into the bottom of the valley. Cross another stile and turn right over a narrow bridge of stone slabs under which the stream gently flows. Continue through the lower part of St. Mary's Vale and join the road by a small car park.

Follow the road down hill for a few hundred yards and take the next turning on the left which leads around the lower slopes of the Rholben spur. Look out for a path ascending the bank on the left, past a National Trust 'Sugar Loaf' sign. This is the traditional Rholben spur route. Engage low gear for a short but stiff climb up the end of the ridge.

Skirrid Fawr pokes his nose up over the Deri and reminds you that he is await-ing your visit. Then Sugar Loaf summit suddenly rises up like a Jack-in-the-box and this is your immediate objective.

Looking down into valley on the right it is interesting to think that between the Rholben and the Deri there used to be a deer park owned by Abergavenny Priory. It was about 500-600 acres in size and was surrounded by a wall which in part still remains. At the head of the valley stands a house called Park Lodge Farm which was formerly the keeper's residence. The farm lower down the valley is called Porth-y-parc — the Gate of the Park.

Rholben is a satisfying ridge route for it provides a direct approach to the summit. About 100 feet below the summit look out for an amazing spring. It is remarkable how so much water can run out of the hill with so little ground above it.

Touch the trig' point (596 metres) and pause for a while to take in the view which according to John White is *'so vast and extensive that it is impossible to attempt a description of it, beyond saying that northwards appear the magnificent range of the Black Mountains above Llanthony; westwards is seen the Blorenge, while between these two points one may succeed on a favourable day, in catching a sight of the Breconshire Beacons; directly south on a clear day the Bristol Channel may be seen and eastwards a beautiful campaign country, rich with green fields and gentle uplands; indeed ten counties - Radnor, Salop, Brecknock, Monmouth, Glamorgan, Worcester, Gloucestershire, Somerset and Wiltshire are more or less visible from this commanding spot.'*

Descend the eastern end of the summit by the stepped path. On reaching a crossing of tracks go right and follow the path heading towards the Deri ridge. It curves around above Cwm Ciby. On reaching a track junction keep right along the crest of the ridge.

After passing over Allt (376 metres) — the highest point on the ridge — the path descends slightly. Bear left at the next junction and follow a broad path down towards a wood. Soon the path narrows and becomes stony, passing be-tween two banks. It then broadens and continues beside a fence passing gnarled and twisted oaks on the right.

Look out for a gate on the left. Go through it and the track then descends between fences. Turn left at a junction and walk past a curious stone archway on the right. Continue along an ancient lane beside a fence and then between mossy stone walls above Triley Court Farm.

On meeting a road turn right and go steeply down to a T junction. Turn left and head for the hamlet of Pant y Gelli. The Crown Inn is very inviting, but don't drink too much for the north face of the Skirrid awaits you! This was once a coaching inn on the old road to Hereford where stage coaches made a brief halt after the long climb out of Abergavenny.

It would seem that 'The Crown' is Britain's most popular inn name and it is sometimes coupled with 'The Rose' and other assorted emblems. Someone once calculated that there are 1,099 Crown Inns scattered around Britain. (It may only be a rough estimate of course, but I don't have the time or inclination to check on the figure.)

Opposite the inn go down the signposted driveway (beside the Pant y Gelli Mission Hall). Follow the drive down to a farm. Opposite the farm house go right over a stone stile. Cross a muddy field (generally churned up by cattle) to reach a stile in the bottom left hand corner. Then continue along a cart track beside a hedge. Go over a stile beside a gate and continue with the hedge now on your right.

Cross a footbridge over the railway and go through a gate. Then cross a low bridge spanning the River Gavenny. Head straight across the next field and cross a stile. Skirrid Fawr is now drawing close but that north face certainly looks steep!

North side of Skirrid Fawr.   *Chris Barber*

Walk across disused section of the old trunk road and then cross the A465 to go up some concrete steps. and cross a stile. Head across a field bearing slightly right to reach a stile. On the other side cross a footbridge spanning a dingle and then turn left along the edge of a field and head up to another stile. Then turn left along a quiet road which is followed for about 1¼ miles (it seems endless!) The 'awesome' profile of Skirrid Fawr looms above.

Archdeacon Coxe was of the opinion that *'the most singular and interesting mountain in the neighbourhood is the the Great Skyrrid, or St. Michael's Mount, which stretches from north to south, or more accurately from north-east to south-west: it is an isolated mount, rising abruptly from the plain; the north-eastern side appears the steep ridge of a brown hue; towards the south and south-east, it slopes gradually into cultivation. The summit is covered with heath, or russet herbage, and its feet are clothed with wood or enriched with corn and pasture.'*

The farm called Llwyn Franc (Frank's Grove) belonged in the 17th century to the Morgan family whose most famous member was Captain Morgan the pirate.

When the road flattens out after the long uphill stretch look out on the right for a stile and footpath sign by a gate (just before a cottage). Go over the stile and head straight up a field to reach another stile to the left of a ruined stone building. Then cross a stream and go through a gate. Head straight across the next field and go over a stile beside a gate. Walk up the next field with a fence and gully on your right. At the top of the field go over a stile beside a gate. Then continue up the next field bearing slightly right. Make for the top right hand corner of the field and go through a small gate.

From here there is a choice of routes up the north slope of Skirrid Fawr. The greater challenge will be found by going right and making for the steep path that ascends the slope directly below the summit. Alternatively, particularly if you are by any chance feeling weary at this point make for the far easier 'Pilgrims' Path'. which goes up to the left. Head for the prominent tree on the skyline directly above.

Just above the tree you will be able to pick up a gently ascending path. (Note — not the one going straight up from here, but the path contouring around to the left). It leads you steadily up the slope with surprisingly little effort involved. On gaining the ridge, turn right and make for the summit (486 metres).

Now descend the long ridge enjoying the splendid views on either side. Sugar Loaf nods to you and you smile and think to yourself 'Yes, I know you well, for I have walked all your ridges and know the intimate secrets of your hidden valleys.' Blorenge broods over Abergavenny and the relentless ascent of that north face seems but a distant memory. Was it really only this morning that you made that climb ? It seems days ago. Ahead can be seen the conical tree covered Skirrid Fach. It only looks a mole hill and you will no doubt experience a feeling of satisfaction that the day's route is nearing its completion.

Drop down off the end of the ridge and go over the stile in the wall to follow the stepped path down through the woods. Cross another stile and walk down the wide track between fences to reach another stile and the B4521.

Turn left and follow the road for about 200 yards. Cross with care and go over a stile beside a gate (near a house). Walk up the field, keeping a hedge on yor left. At the top of the field go over a stile and turn left along a path running between two fences. Go over a stile at the end of it and shortly turn right along a road which leads through the hamlet of Bryngwenin.

At the end of the road go left over a stile next to a gate. Now head straight across field to another stile — straight across next field to a stile — then on beside a fence — over a stile — cross a field — over a stile. Looking back now, Skirrid Fawr looks like a slumbering whale.

Cross a road and go down the concrete drive to Ty Draw Farm. Keep straight on through a farmyard and then walk on between hedges following a cart track to reach a gate. Cross a stream and bear right across a field to pass through a gateway. Head directly across the next field to reach a stile. Turn right and follow the B4233. Shortly, cross the road and go over a stile by a footpath sign.

Bear slightly right across the field to reach a stile above a dingle. Cross the stile and a stream, then ascend a bank and continue along the edge of a field, keeping a hedge on your left. The path roughly follows a line of pylons. Go over a stile and continue through the next field. Ignore the next stile on the left. Walk past the next pylon, cross a ditch and go over a stile. Cross the next field and head for its left hand corner to go through a gate by a footpath sign. Turn right along a road.

Follow the road uphill and where it flattens out turn right. From here there is a good view across to the Blorenge. Keep straight on at the next junction. The track now heads up through the trees. Ignore a right turning and also one on the left. The gradient steepens and then suddenly you emerge from the trees into a small clearing on the summit of Skirrid Fach, your seventh summit! Its true Welsh name is Ysgyryd Fach and the summit plateau is 300 metres above sea level.

Skirrid Fach from across the River Usk.   *Chris Barber*

Years ago this used to be a popular walk for Abergavenny people and there used to be a flag pole on the summit. Unfortunately the trees have matured and the once excellent view is no longer available. Archdeacon Coxe climbed this hill in 1799 and more than adequately described the view. We cannot see it now due to the height of the trees so we will have take his word for what he saw.

'This prospect is the most delightful,and elegant in Monmouthshire: it is suffici-ently distant to produce the effect of landscape; yet not so extensive as to render the objects indistinct. Beneath, the vale stretches from Crickhowell to the Clytha hills, watered by the Usk, meandering through rich tracts of corn, pasture. and wood, occasionally lost in the midst of thickets, and again bursting into view. Above the right bank of this beautiful river, extends the chain of wooded eminences, from the

extremity of the Blorenge to the rich groves of Pontypool Park; from the left sweeps the fertile district in which the mansions of Clytha, Llanarth and Llansantfraed are situated. The distant and cultivated parts of Herefordshire present themselves on each side of the majestic and independent Skyrrid. To the west of the Skyrrid, rises an enormous mass of mountains; among which are most conspicuous the long line of the Black Mountains, the russet top of the Brynaro, the towering point of the Sugar Loaf, and the magnificent swell of the Blorenge. The four undulating eminences which support the Sugar Loaf are particularly discriminated, and Abergavenny seated, at their feet, is seen to the greatest advantage. As we caught a bird's-eye view of the town, with its white houses illuminated by the rays of a meridian sun, and relieved by the surrounding verdue, it appeared like the picture of a camera obscura.'

Go straight across the summit and follow a stepped path down through the trees. It descends through a dense wood and crosses several tracks that encircle the hill. In due course you will reach a stile at the bottom of the wood. Continue beside a hedge and then cross another stile. Abergavenny is now spread out below.

Head straight down to join a fence and then walk on beside a stream. Go over a stile, cross a footbridge and continue through the next field. Cross the last stile of the day and with considerable care negotiate the most dangerous part of the route - the crossing of the A465, Turn right and after a few yards go left by a footpath sign to follow a path beside a fence which leads to a footbridge over the railway line. You have now arrived at Abergavenny Railway Station.

Abergavenny Railway Station. It was at this station on the morning of Monday 2nd January 1854 that Abergavenny welcomed its first passenger train. Down 'the bank' from Llanfihangel it clanked to a rather squeaky stop at the 'station' of the Newport, Abergavenny and Hereford Railway. The first stationmaster was Mr. Jos Peake and according to his contract he was expected to live on the premises and be available for duty 365 days of the year.

Follow the pavement down to the Monmouth Road and then turn right to walk back to Abergavenny and your starting point.

SUGGESTED TIME SCHEDULE

Start in Abergavenny	*8.00a.m.*
Summit of Blorenge	*9.30a.m.*
Glangrwyne	*11.15a.m.*
Llanwenarth Breast	*12.45p.m.*
Rholben	*1.30p.m.*
Sugar Loaf summit	*2.00p.m.*
Pant-y-Gelli	*2.45p.m.*
Skirrid Fawr	*4.15p.m.*
Skirrid Fach	*5.15p.m.*
Abergavenny	*6.15p.m.*

BLORENGE

'The ugly, loutish, brutish head of the Blorenge, capped like its fellows the Llangattwg and Llangynidir ranges, with millstone grit, by pushing aggressively in upon the Usk from the south completes the ring of mountains that girdle the town.'
H.J. Massingham — 'The Southern Marches'

Llanfoist Bridge and The Blorenge.   Chris Barber

A friend of mine once remarked to me that in his opinion the Blorenge is a boring mountain and that he had no interest in visiting its summit. I found myself disagreeing quite strongly with his point of view and went on to describe in detail some of the fascinating walks that are possible on this hill which sits like an armchair overlooking Abergavenny. Sometimes it seems to frown on the town, but on a summer evening, when its northern slopes are just catching the evening light, it forms a serene and beautiful backcloth.

Many visits are necessary before you can begin to know the Blorenge, for this hill unfolds its secrets very gradually to the walker who roams the tracks and tramroads, pondering on its range of antiquities dating from prehistoric times to the age of the Industrial Revolution. No! the Blorenge is never boring; tiring certainly, if you tackle its steep north face, but once you begin to understand its hidden qualities you will return time and time again.

The name Blorenge is often queried by visitors and locals alike. It does not sound a Welsh name and it has been suggested that the original Welsh was perhaps Blorens. One writer suggests that it came from Blawreng and that it means grey or blue ridge. Local people used to firmly believe that the hill is full of water and one day it will burst forth and drown Abergavenny !

John White, who wrote a guide book to the area in 1877, observed that *'The Blorenge is rendered interesting on many accounts. It forms a termination to the great mineral basin of South Wales, and is situated on what was formerly termed "The Wilds of Monmouthshire." Here terminates the valley Afon Llwyd, named from the stream running through it. From its bowels, the Blaenavon, the Garnddyrys, and in some measure, the Nantyglo Ironworks, extract their wealth.'*

When I look at the symmetrical hulk of the Blorenge from Abergavenny I always think of a blancmange for it has the appearance of being tipped out of a giant mould. There is even an impression of majesty in the way that it dominates the southern side of the town but when seen from the east it appears merely as an abrupt termination to a long ridge that stretches from Pontypool.

ROUTE 2

AROUND THE SUMMIT PLATEAU (4 miles, 2 hours)

'The Blorenge reaches the very respecatable height of 1834 feet, with a fine plateau several miles long sloping southwards.'

N.G. Brett-James

Start from Foxhunter car park (SO 263107).

Before commencing the walk pay a visit to the grave containg the hideof a remarkable horse who gave his name to this car park. A narrow path leads to a rock outcrop where you will find a plaque bearing the following inscription:

3rd April 1940 - 21st November 1959
Here lies Foxhunter
Champion International Show Jumper

Winner of 78 International Competitions, including many foreign Grand Prix and the King George V Gold Cup 1948, 1950 and 1953.
35 times member of the British Show Jumping team which won Olympic Medal at Helsinki 1952.
Bronze medals at London 1948, Prince of Wales Cup, London, five times (1949-1953) and the Aga Khan Cup outright, Dublin (1950, 1951-1953).

Now follow a well trodden track across the moorland, past occasional stone cairns to reach the Blorenge summit. (559 metres). Here you will find a trig' point and a large cairn of stones. Pause to take in the extensive view and see how many summits you can identify. On a clear day the main peaks of the Brecon Beacons will be recognised on the western horizon.

Continue along a path which goes past the cairn and across the moorland to reach the north east slopes of the hill. Head down to a little square brick building close to the edge of the steep north east escarpment of the Blorenge.

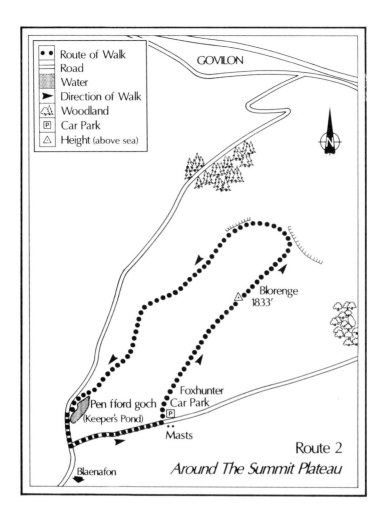

Here on a clear day you will enjoy a bird's eye view of Abergavenny, the Vale of Usk, Sugar Loaf, Black Mountains, Skirrid Fawr, Skirrid Fach and in the far distance you may even pick out the Malvern Hills.

Hang-gliding enthusiasts come to this escarpment when the wind conditions are favourable, to launch themselves into space. It is one of the highest sites in the country regularly used by hang- glider pilots and their flight down to Castle Meadows on the other side of the river must be an exhilarating experience.

Now contour around the lip of the escarpment to the left. Maintain height, enjoying panoramic views up through the Usk Valley towards Crickhowell. Then descend slightly to pass through a shallow gully and join an old tram road which gently crosses the hillside and leads you to Keeper's Pond, otherwise known as Pen-fford-goch Pond.

Keeper's Pond with Sugar Loaf in the distance.   *Chris Barber*

This is a popular spot in summer but on a cold windy day you will probably have it to yourself. The pond was constructed as a water supply for the Blaenafon Ironworks on one side of the hill and Garnddyrys Forge on the other. Early Ordnance Survey maps refer to it as Forge Pond and it was established here about 1820.

From the Pond you may either make your way back to the starting point by following sheep tracks across the tufty country to the left or make your way up to a road which leads to the Foxhunter car park.

ROUTE 3

UP THE INCLINE (3½ miles, 3 hours)

'The tramroad runs almost evenly with the edge of the Blorenge to the side of Cwm Craf, where pulleys, wheels and iron chains liberate the trams loaded with coal, iron and limestone down the terrible slope to their first resting situation, where a similar apparatus dispatches them onwards to the second stage, and then another to the third on the Brecon and Abergavenny canal.'

Thomas Evan Watkins

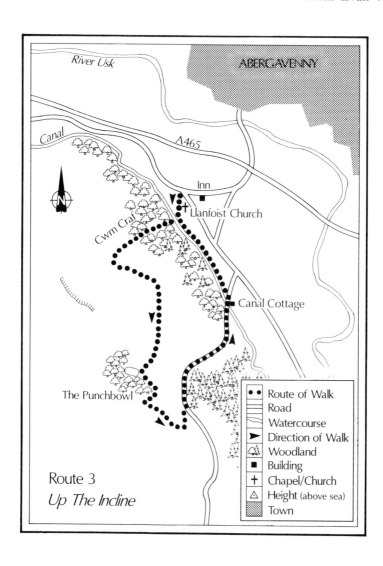

Route 3
Up The Incline

● ●	Route of Walk
	Road
	Watercourse
►	Direction of Walk
🔺	Woodland
■	Building
+	Chapel/Church
△	Height (above sea)
	Town

Park in Llanfoist near the lych gate of St. Faith's Church, alongside the stone wall. To reach this spot you have to turn up Kiln Lane, beside the Llanfoist Inn (One Way System) and then go right at the T junction at the top of a short rise. The lych gate to the church is then shortly on your left.

Go through the lych gate and into Llanfoist Churchyard. A good way of gaining an insight into the history of any village is to take a good look around its graveyard. Well, this one is really fascinating with memorial stones and tombs that help to tell the story of the people who lived and worked in this area during the last two hundred years.

The correct Welsh for Llanfoist is Llanffwyst and it would seem that Ffwyst was a priest of the monastic college of Seriol, a saint who lived in Anglesey in the 6th century. He is reputed to have founded the first church on this site. The present building is a reconstruction of a 13th century church which is described in one old book as having a 'barn-like appearance.' A brass inside the church informs the visitor that: 'This church was restored to the praise and glory of God in memory of the late Crawshay Bailey, esquire of Llanfoist House, by his affectionate son Crawshay Bailey of Maindiff Court, Abergavenny A.D. Oct 1873.'

Crawshay Bailey Senior is buried in the churchyard. You will find it difficult to miss his grave for it is the one with the tall shiny pillar. He is probably the most famous of all the ironmasters and with his brother Joseph developed one of the largest ironworks in the world at Nantyglo. In addition he also found time to build railways, sink pits and play a part in the construction of canals. Later in his life he turned to politics and became Member of Parliament for Monmouthshire and Newport Borough. On his retirement he lived in Llanfoist House and was 83 years old when he passed away.

Continue up the lane and where it bends to the left, go right to pass through a tunnel beneath the canal. When the canal was being constructed, this tunnel was included as a part of the engineering works to allow the old parish road to continue along this route. This subterranean way is 40 yards long and approximately 6 feet wide and 7 feet high — but most people will automatically duck their heads.

Above the tunnel is the old Wharfmaster's House and nearby is Hill's Warehouse, which has in recent years been converted into a very attractive residence. Llanfoist wharf was once a very busy place, for it was here that the trams from Garnddyrys were unloaded and the iron and coal transferred to the waiting barges for the two day journey to Newport Docks. Barges heading in the other direction, took coal and lime to Brecon.

Keep straight on, to cross a stile and head up through the woods beside a stream. You are now about to ascend a section of the Llanfoist Incline which used to be known as 'The Big Drop.' As you puff your way upwards look out for stones with holes bored into them which were used as sleepers to support the double line of rails. Unfortunately very few of them are still in position having been disturbed over the years and tumbled into the stream by thoughtless people unappreciative of their historical importance.

A platform at the top of this slope is where a brake wheel set in a pit, used to control the rate of descent of the trams. A continuous chain was passed around the wheel and fastened to the trams on each line of rails. On some of the stones still in place on the incline it is possible to see grooves cut by the passage of the chain. The platforms between the separate inclines also served as collecting areas where the trams could be arranged in order of priority before being transferred to the next section. Full trams descended under gravity pulling empty ones up on the other track.

Looking down the 'big drop' on the Llanfoist Incline.　　　　*Drawing by Michael Blackmore*

A guide book to Abergavenny, published in 1866 provides an interesting description of the incline tram system that was still in existence at that time. It was no longer in use, but obviously in living memory, people had been using it as a way of ascending the the hillside.

'*At length we arrive at the place where the inclined planes begin to rise up the side of the Blorenge. These at one time afforded great assistance in climbing the steep. The traveller seated himself in a tramcart, and was pulled upwards by the force of the loaded carriages descending, by means of a chain which worked round a wheel at the top. He thus accomplished more than half the distance to the summit of the mountain, a height of 1,720 feet, with little effort on his own part.'*

From the first platform continue past a little brick hut to reach a stile. Further on you will emerge from the woods high up on the hollow of Cwm Craf. At this point the final section of the incline went up at an angle on the right to meet Hill's Tramroad on the hillside above. There is no right of way up that section of incline, so you keep going straight up to reach another stile. Pause here to catch your breath and take in the view over Abergavenny and the Usk Valley.

Thomas Evan Watkins in his 'History of Llanfoist' claimed that *'in times of persecution it is said that people were placed on top of this valley in a kind of wooden barrel, tied and closed up, the barrel peneytrated with nails, and then rolled topsy turvy, headlong down to the bottom.'*

On the other side of the stile, follow a track beside the fence to the left around the shoulder of the Blorenge. The view to the left over Abergavenny towards the Sugar Loaf and Skirrid Fawr is very impressive. Go through a gate and on beside the fence. Then ascend slightly through the next field and suddenly before you in a lovely hollow known as the Punchbowl is a man-made lake. This natural depression is called in Welsh Taren Cwn y Dison and it is of glacial origin. When the atmospheric conditions are suitable you will find that this location has exceptional accoustic qualities. The sheep will no doubt think you mad, but try shouting across the water at the hill side above and listen to the echo.

Years ago this was a secret meeting place for mountain fighters who used to come here to participate in prize- fighting contests. They fought with bare fists and proudly wore the scars of previous fights on their broken-nosed faces. A look out was always posted, for the sport was illegal. The spectators who came here to watch the fun and place bets, used to quietly make their way up the incline from Llanfoist and follow tracks around the hillside to reach the Punchbowl.

Stories are sometimes told of a fight that once took place in 1889 between David Rees of Nantyglo and William Williams of Brynmawr for the handsome sum of £10. The affair was kept quiet although the combatants had for the past two weeks been preparing for the fight.

It proved an exciting contest but at the close of the 42nd round . . . yes 42nd! . . . Rees threw in the sponge and Williams was declared the winner. The fight had lasted 1 hour 27 minutes. However the result was not considered satisfactory to many of the spectators and a number of angry minor fights followed !

In the woods above the Punchbowl lake is an outcrop of Old Red Sandstone which at one time was quarried and crushed into sand for use in the local ironworks.

Bear left and go up beside a stone wall. On reaching a field at the top of the slope, go left to join a sunken lane which leads down to a road. Turn right and follow the road to a T junction. Go left here and immediately cross a stile to follow a fence down to a gate on the edge of a forestry plantation. Contine along a gravel track down through the trees to reach a lane leading to a stone bridge over the canal. Cross a stone stile on the right and join the canal towpath. Follow the towpath back to Llanfoist Wharf.

ROUTE 4

HILL'S TRAMROAD (3½ miles, 3 hours)

This is a linear walk starting from Keeper's Pond Car Park and finishing at Llanfoist. It is recommended that you position an additional car at the end of the walk at a suitable spot in Llanfoist village and then drive to the starting point in the other car(s). Otherwise catch a Blaenafon bus and alight at Keeper's Pond.

The Welsh name for this pond is Pen-fford-goch which means 'Pond at the head of the red road' and it would seem that when the Blaenafon to Abergavenny road was being constructed in 1825 by the Blaenafon Ironworks Company, Old Red Sandstone which occurs in this vicinity was was crused and used as a surface material. The red colour of the road was made even more apparent when red ash from the Garnddyrys furnaces was used for repair work.

The pond later became known as 'Keeper's Pond' after the Keeper's Cottage which used to stand nearby. This little stone cottage was demolished in about 1970. The Keeper's job was to manage the Blorenge grouse moors which are the most southerly in Britain.

Hill's Tramroad at the head of Cwm Ifor.   *Drawing by Michael Blackmore*

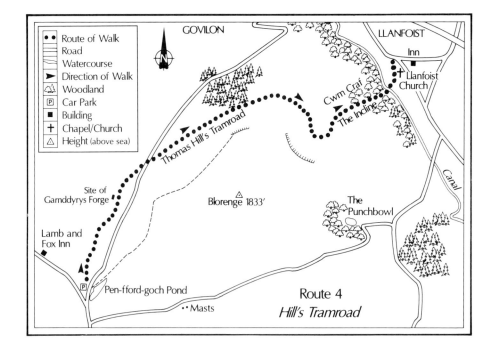

Route 4
Hill's Tramroad

On the other side of the road, below the pond follow a track down from a Footpath Signpost. Shortly go right to descend into the head of Cwm Llanwenarth down a track that becomes a rocky ledge. It is known as Rhiw Ifor (Ifor's track) but just who Ifor was is something of a mystery.It would seem that he was certainly someone of importance way back in the very distant past for his name crops up in several places in this area. On the hillside above is Croes Ifor (Ifor's Cross) and near by is a heap of stones referred to as Ifor's Castle. There is also a location called Cwm Ifor (Ifor's Dingle).

At the bottom of the rocky slope turn right along the broad track of Hill's Tramroad. This fascinating route was engineered by Thomas Hill in about 1825 when a tramroad of 2 feet 0 inches gauge was built to connect the Blaenafon Ironworks with the Brecon and Abergavenny Canal at Llanfoist. It conveyed iron, coal and limestone. At a rough estimate it was in operation for a period of just under 30 years and probably closed in about 1853. Thomas Hill built it in two stages. The first section was constructed at some time before 1819 to carry limestone to the blast furnaces at Blaenafon. Pig iron and coal was also conveyed to the Garnddyrys Forge. The refined iron was then taken back along the tramroad to Blaenafon and conveyed down the valley to the Monmouthshire Canal at Pontypool.

This was a tedious journey and it was obviously more desirable to make use of the Brecon and Abergavenny Canal at Llanfoist, which would shorten the route considerably. So a second stage of the tramroad was constructed in 1824-25 from the Garnddyrys Forge to follow the 1200 foot contour around to the north side of the Blorenge. From there three inclined planes were built to descend Cwm Craf to enable the trams to be lowered to the canal wharf at Llanfoist. A further extension of the tramroad on a bridge spanning the canal connected with a fourth incline which descended to Llanfoist Coal Yard and lime kilns.

Cross the stream at the head of Cwm Ifor where the old tramroad bridge has collapsed and continue past the remains of a little building where horses were once shod and then on above a steep slope known as the Tumble. You will observe stones set into the track with holes bored into them. Iron saddles were fastened to these blocks to secure the rails which were fixed in place by spikes driven into wooden plugs inserted in the block holes. The L shaped cast iron rails were designed to guide smooth and non-flanged wheels and were 4 feet long, 3 inches deep, 2½ inches wide and chamfered to 2 inches wide on the top running surface.

The 'monster' slag heap at Garnddyrys.   Chris Barber

Ahead now you will see a strange looking heap of dark material which resembles a prehistoric monster. This is the main slag dump and it has been shaped by over a century of wind and rain into this form.

Leave the track which heads down past the towering pile of slag and walk across a level strip of land where the Garnddyrys Iron Forge once stood. Today, only the foundations of a few buildings can be seen and stonework in the bank on the right, above which was once a reservoir.

The Garnddyrys Forge and Rolling Mill were only in operation for about fifty years and situated here at an altitude of 1,300 feet this seems a most unlikely site for an industrial undertaking. The narrow strip of land was in fact purchased in 1817 from William Price for £75 and by siting the forge here it was conveniently placed between Blaenafon and Llanfoist Wharf on the Brecknock and Abergavenny Canal.

A re-construction of Garnddyrys Forge, featured by Alexander Cordell in his novel 'Rape of the Fair Country', and now brought to life through the pen of Michael Blackmore. This is how it may have looked in about 1850.

This little hillside forge turned out some 300 tons of finished products in a typical week's operation and it is of interest that the wrought iron for Crumlin Viaduct was produced here in the 1850's. By 1860 the railway had arrived in Blaenafon and the decision was taken to dismantle the plant at Garnddyrys and move the rolling mill to a new works at Forgeside on the Coity Mountain side of Blaenafon.

There is little evidence now of the forge and rolling mill that once stood on this spot. The main feature is the retaining wall above where an outlet to the upper pond can be seen. This was approximately one acre in area and supplied water for powering steam engines on the site.

Further on, to your left you will pass the site of the Garnddyrys Square which consisted of 20 houses built on three sides of a rectangle providing 5, 10 and 5 houses on each side. It seems amazing now to think that some 300 people used to live in the vicinity of Garnddyrys and their cottages are now just piles of stone.

Go up to the road and follow it down for about 100 yards and then cross it and continue along Hill's Tramroad. At this point used to stand the Queen Victoria Inn which was frequented by the workers of Garnddyrys. A humorous story is often told of a man who bought this inn just before the second world war and carried out certain improvements to it, including the installation of electric light.

One night he held a lively party to celebrate and whilst someone was thumping a rowdy song out on the piano, the floor gave way and everyone including the piano fell into the cellar.

Soon you will reach a shallow cutting which leads to a tunnel. Adventurous walkers will choose to scramble down into it and walk though to the other side. If this does not appeal to you then follow the track over the top enjoying the open views over the Usk Valley to the Black Moutains.

In due course as you round a corner into the hollow on the north side of the Blorenge you will see a retaining wall on the right. It was at this point that the first section of incline descended on the left into Cwm Craf. It is not a right of way so you will have to continue along a track beside the fence and then head down towards a stile. From here head straight down towards the trees and follow a path leading steeply down through the wooded valley, shortly joining the next stage of the incline. Go over a stile and then on down to a platform where you will see a small brick hut. From here the incline descends very steeply and this section is known as 'The Big Drop.'

An interesting description of its operation is provided by Thomas Evan Watkins in His 'History of Llanfoist' written in 1834.

'The tramroad runs almost evenly with the edge of the Blorenge to the side of Cwmcraf, where pulleys, wheels and iron chains liberate the trams, loaded with coal, iron and limestone, down the terrible slope to their first resting station, where a similar apparatus dispatches them onwards to their second stage, and then another to the third on the Brecon and Abergavenny canal bank, and likewise the loaded trams bring the empty ones up the steepy heights on the side of Cwm Craf to the canal. Here they unload the trams and fill the boats with iron etc for the port of Newport-on-Usk to meet the ships which sail from pole to pole to all the harbours of the habitable Globe.'

At the bottom of the incline go over a stile and walk straight on to enter a tunnel which passes beneath the Wharf Master's House and the canal. The noise of your boots echos off the walls and mixes with the sound of a gurgling stream which flows into a gully on the right. The tunnel is 40 yards long and about 6 feet wide and 7 feet high. It was constructed for pedestrian use and enabled the tram road and incline operators who lived in Llanfoist to walk to work.

If you wish to see the Llanfoist Wharf go up some steps on the left to emerge on the canal towpath opposite Hill's Warehouse, which is known locally as the Boathouse. This wharf was once a bustling scene of activity where the trams loaded with iron, coal and limestone descended the inclines and their loads were transferred to the waiting barges. From here iron and coal was taken on a two-day journey to Newport Docks and Lime and coal went in the other direction to Brecon.

It was a complex operation for the traffic was in both directions. For example, high quality Spanish ore was brought by barge from Newport and then sent up the incline to Garnddyrys and then on through the Pwll-du tunnel to Blaenafon. It later returned through the tunnel as pig iron en route for Garnddyrys to be refined and then finally descended the incline to Llanfoist as a finished product.

Continue down the lane and return to your starting point.

ROUTE 5

ASCENT FROM GOVILON (5¼ miles, 3½ hours)

'The ascent of the Blorenge from this western side is rather steep, and the natives advise caution and possibly a friend to guide you.'

N.G. Brett-James

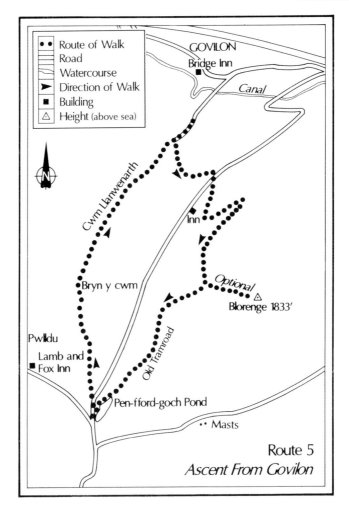

Route 5
Ascent From Govilon

Starting from the Bridgend Inn follow Church Lane past the church and pass under a low canal bridge. On the other side ascend a flight of steps on the left. Go over a stile and walk on beside a fence. You will notice a series of canal boundary posts on the left, inscribed 'Great Western Railway.'

At the end of the fence the track drops down to a stream and passes through an attractive dingle. Cross the stream on a narrow footbridge and then walk through a field to ascend a stepped path up a bank, which leads to a stile.

Turn left along a road and shortly go right over a bridge spanning the old Abergavenny to Merthyr railway line. Then immediately turn right again. Keep straight on at the next junction to pass the old School House on your right.

On reaching a house on the left called Mount Pleasant, go up a track on the far side of it. At a bend just before another house, follow the narrow path up to the right. It continues up the hillside between stone walls and with your feet crunching on the leaves of countless autumns you pass beautiful beech trees to shortly look down on the village of Govilon. Then go steeply up to meet the Blaenafon road. Cross it and go straight up the bank on the other side and over a stile.

Continue beside a stone wall to shortly reach another stile. Then walk on with the wall now on your left to a third stile. Follow the path to the left to join a stone wall and fence and then continue up the slope to reach the corner of a plantation. Then after a few yards follow a diagonal path up to the right which brings you onto Hill's Tramroad, where you turn left.

On reaching a double line of holed stones, shortly go up a diagonal path on the right which doubles back on itself. This will lead you gently up through the bracken. Soon you are looking back down to the tramroad and into Cwm Llanwenarth. The views also open up through the Usk Valley towards Crickhowell.

In due course you join a higher tramroad and here you have a choice of route. Either continue directly upwards following indistinct sheep paths to reach the summit of the Blorenge (and then make your way along the plateau and down to Keeper's Pond) or turn right here and follow this tramroad around to Keeper's Pond.

From Keeper's Pond descend to the Blaenafon road and by a footpath sign, follow a broad track for about 100 yards. Then walk down the track on the right (Rhiw Ifor). Soon you are looking down on Hill's Tramroad once more. Descend a rocky ramp flanked by a weather worn limestone outcrop. Go straight across the tramroad and follow a path down into Cwm Llanwenarth.

A gate is reached and the track continues between moss covered stone walls. On the right you will notice the remains of old cottages that were once occupied by people who worked at the Garnddyrys Forge. This lovely old track brings you down into the bottom of the valley where you join the tumbling stream.

Cross a little stone bridge and bear left to follow the main path beside the stream. Shortly you reach another gate and then continue through this peaceful valley. In due course the track joins a road. Keep straight on passing some attractive stone cottages. At the end of the lane you rejoin your outward route.

Cross the bridge over the old railway and turn right (for a different route back to the start). Shortly you pass the Station Master's House (Old Govilon Station). Go over a footbridge spanning the canal, turn right and follow the towpath under the footbridge and the stone bridge. Shortly, you cross a small aqueduct, and around the next corner descend some stone steps on the right. Follow the road down to the Bridgend Inn at Govilon.

The name Govilon may be a corruption of gefaillon which means forges and this is significant for at one time there were several at this location.

MYNYDD PEN Y FAL (Sugar Loaf)

'It rises, like Vesuvius, to the clouds, describing an outline remarkable for its undeviating smoothness and easy graduation.'

John White 1877

The Sugar Loaf and Abergavenny.   *Chris Barber*

Most people know this distinctive hill as the Sugar Loaf and its Welsh name is rarely heard these days, so I will refer to it by its English name. For those readers who have not been to Abergavenny, the Sugar Loaf is a conical shaped hill and it is unmistakeable as you approach the town. However from a distance when seen from certain angles it is sometimes confused with Skirrid Fawr and vice versa.

It is certainly a landmark that can be seen from a many miles away and it is a seductive summit that entices even folk who are not usually walkers. They can of course cheat a little and drive their cars up to the high-level car park on Llanwenarth Breast. From there a comparatively easy grassy path leads up to the summit. It is only the last few hundred feet that are steep, but as long as one doesn't try to go too fast the ascent is accomplished with relative ease, even if you are normally just a 'walk the dog in the park' rambler.

From a distance the summit looks small and flat but it is suprisingly long when you get there. It is really a narrow ridge about three hundred yards long with a cluster of rocks at the western end.

There are of course numerous ways of ascending this hill for it has three southern offshoots: the Deri, Rholben and Mynydd Llanwenarth, with valleys in between, and routes to the summit are possible using all these approaches. You can also tackle it from Fforest Coalpit on the north east side, or from the village of Llanbedr in the north west; or Llangenny or Glangrwyney.

Whatever route you choose, you will not be disappointed but the Sugar Loaf always seems to be a much higher hill than its height suggests, for the approaches (with the exception of the 'cheat route') are quite long. The summit is 1,955 feet above sea level or 596 metres if you prefer the metric equivalent. Sadly the Sugar Loaf fails to attain the magic figure of 2,000 feet which to some walkers is the necessary qualification for mountain status. But never mind for when you get to the top it feels like a mountain and you can certainly see lots of mountains from it!

In 1909 Wade's guide book provided the following description of the Sugar Loaf:-

'Its altitude, its striking individuality and its unobstructed situation makes it one of the most easily recognisable features in the Monmouthshire landscape. Its name perfectly suggests its appearance. At a distance it seems to swell up-wards from the plain in a single graceful cone: but on a nearer view it reveals itself to be by no means so simply constructed a mountain as it appears. The cone really rests upon the backs of four globular hills which are divided from it by a depression. Three of these supporters, the Deri, the Rholben, and Mynydd Llanwenarth, as seen from Abergavenny stand directly in front, and a further spur projects in the rear. The pretty wooded sides of its supporters make a fine foil to the smooth and shapely swell of the cone above.

'The actual height of the mountain is 1955 feet, and it need hardly be said that the view from the top is magnificent. The panorama is most extensive and embraces practically the whole of the county and a large portion of the neighbouring shires of Brecon and Hereford. The Malvern Hills on the N.E. the Shropshire Hills and the Black Mountains on the N., and the Breconshire Beacons on the N.W., are easily identified among the more distant eminences. The neighbouring heights of the Skyrrid and the Blorenge are in full view, and on a very clear day the Somerset and Devonshire hills, the Cotswolds and the Wiltshire Downs are also within the field of vision.'

At the turn of the century Buffalo Bill brought his Wild West show to Abergavenny and the Sugar Loaf obviously caught his eye for he decided to take a walk up to its summit. Apparently half the town went with him!

ROUTE 6

THE EASY WAY (4 miles, 2 hours)

'The mountaineer's best answer to anyone who asks, "Why do you climb?" is simply "Because I like it".'

F.S. Smythe.

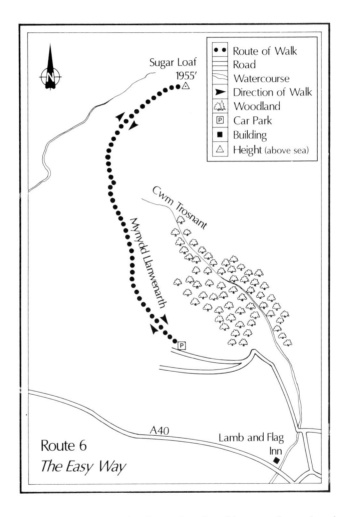

This is the shortest route up the Sugar Loaf and it starts from the viewpoint car park at SO 268167. This is reached by turning right from the A40 into Pentre Lane about half a mile west of Abergavenny. Follow the signs directing you to the Sugar Loaf.

From the car park which provides an excellent view, a well defined track leads along the curved ridge of Mynydd Llanwenarth and ascends the Sugar Loaf by the south-west slope.

Looking towards the Black Mountains from Sugar Loaf.   *Chris Barber*

'During my continuance on the summit, I felt that extreme satisfaction which I always experience when elevated on the highest point of the circumjacent country. The air is more pure, the body more active, and the mind more serene; lifted above the dwellings of man, we discard all grovelling and earthly passions; the thoughts assume a character of sublimity, proportionate to the grandeur of the surrounding objects and as the body approaches nearer to the ethereal regions, the soul imbibes a portion of their unalterable purity.'

Archdeacon William Coxe

Return to the car park by the same route.

ROUTE 7

UP ST. MARY'S VALE AND DOWN THE RHOLBEN
(4¼ miles, 3 hours)

'*The Rholben and the Deri leaning against the Sugar Loaf like flying butresses, do not in the least obscure its nobility of outline nor diminish the sense of loftiness it imparts. Islanded by streams, the Grwyne Fawr, the Usk and the Gavenny, its turfy slopes soar upwards in ogee curves to the pyramidal top with its cap of quartzite visible from below. Not a line falters; Rholben and Deri are merely the train of this priestly mount. There are many sugar-loaf mountains in South Wales but there is only one Sugar Loaf*'.

H.J. Massingham

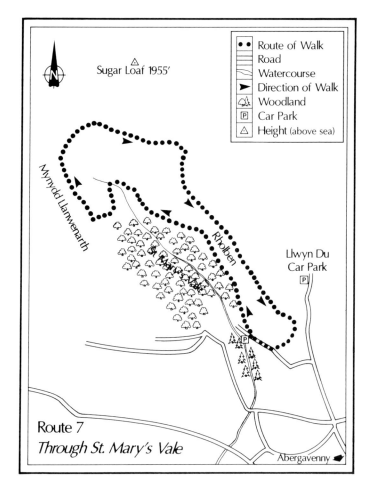

This walk starts from a small car park situated at the entrance to St. Mary's Vale.

Leaving the car park, follow the rising track to the left. On reaching a hairpin bend keep straight on following the stony track up through the trees. It climbs steadily above the deep valley and is well shaded by overhanging trees.

In due course you will emerge from the trees to obtain a good view down into the wooded valley on the left. This is the 'ravine' of Nant Iago which is inappropriately known as St. Mary's Vale. It has no connection with the saint and is not a vale but a deep narrow and thickly wooded dell.

When you reach a track junction, keep to the left and go over a stile to pass through a fenced area (where the National Trust are endeavouring to encourage new tree growth).

Bear left at a junction and shortly go over a stile in a fence. The path now descends slightly and crosses a stream. Here is a pleasant spot for a picnic beneath two oak trees. Further on the track descends gently towards the head of the valley. Cross a stream gully and walk on to reach the head of the valley where another stream is joined.

Cross the stream and follow it for about 50 yards. Then turn up a well-used track ascending the slope on the left. On joining the crest of the ridge turn right along a broad path. From here you can look directly across to the summit of the Sugar Loaf where the trig' point is clearly visible.

At the next junction follow the track to the right, descending slightly and curving around the head of the valley. On reaching a crossing of tracks continue to the right, now heading in the direction of the Sugar Loaf summit.

Looking down St. Mary's Vale on the right, Skirrid Fach can be seen in the distance and the tower of St. Mary's priory church.

Turn right at the next crossing of tracks and follow a path descending the Rholben ridge. Cross a stream and continue, ignoring a path on the left. Turn right at the next junction and walk on down the ridge enjoying the view towards southern Gwent with the Severn glinting in the distance.

At the end of the ridge Abergavenny can be seen spread out below. From here the path leads steeply down passing a metal seat on the way. This was placed here many years ago for the benefit of Sugar Loaf walkers by the Abergavenny Public Footpath and Neighbourhood Improvement Society. At a meeting in June 1883 the following works were reported to be successfully carried out:-

'The Sugar Loaf carriage drive with stable erected during the climb to the summit of the mountain; the Sugar Loaf footpath, making the ascent to the peak easy for old and young and such as are not accustomed to climbing over rocky crags; the Rholben footpath by which the early stages to the Sugar Loaf are accomplished without fatigue. In fact, so nicely laid out are both paths that safe ascent may now be made by families with ponies or donkeys to carry the children with provisions etc. . . . By the footpath side several seats have been fixed and it is contemplated to provide more if funds are forthcoming.'

On joining a road, follow it down to a T junction and turn right. Go up the road and return to the car park.

ROUTE 8

THE BACK DOOR ROUTE (6½ miles, 3½ hours)

'When we reach the mountain summits we leave behind us all the things that weigh heavily down below on our body and spirit. We leave behind all sense of weakness and depression. We feel a new freedom, a great exhilaration, an exhaltation of the body no less than of the spirit. We feel a great joy.'

J.C. Smutts

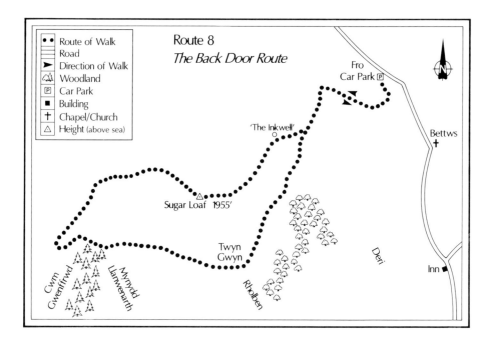

This walk starts from Ffro car park at SO 291201. It is reached by turning off the old Hereford road at Pant y Gelli. Drive past Bettws and after about a mile you will find the small car park is on the left hand side of the road.

At the rear of the car park a footpath leads to a gate. Then go left beside a fence which soon beconmes a stone wall. When the path divides, follow the right hand track which becomes a broad path. Go over a rise and the Sugar Loaf summit comes into view. To the right can be seen the Gaer hill-fort.

On reaching a T junction by a small cairn, go left and continue beside the stone wall observing the craftmanship of its construction. Skirrid Fawr will now dramatically appear on the left.

After about ¼ mile, go diagonally right along a well-worn path leading up towards some trees. Beyond the trees it steepens and then gradually brings you on to the ridge leading up to the Sugar Loaf summit.

The path now follows a slightly raised edge with a shallow ditch on the left hand side. A small pool is passed on the right, which from above looks like an 'inkwell,' but often drys up in the summer.

In due course the path begins to steepen and the final ascent begins. On reaching the stone steps leading to the summit you know that you are nearly there. Walk along the summit plateau, touch the trig point and admire the view.

The View from this point is magnificent, extensive and diversified. It commands the counties of Radnor, Glamorgan, Hereford, Worcester, Gloucester, Somerset, and Wiltshire. To the west extends the long and beautiful Vale of Usk, winding in the recesses of the mountains, and expanding south into the fertile plain, which is terminated by the Clytha hills. Above it towers the magnificent Blorenge, almost equal in height to the point on which I stood; and in the midst rises the swell of the Little Skrrrid, appearing like a gentle eminence feathered with wood. To the north a bleak, dreary sublime mass of mountains, stretches in a circular range from the extremity of the Black Mountains above Llanthony to the Table Rock near Crickhowell; the commencement of the great chain which extends from these confines of Monmouthshire across North Wales, to the Irish Sea. To the east I looked down on the broken crags of the Great Skyrrid, which starts up in the midst of a rich and cultivated region. Beyond the Malvern Hills, the Graig, the Garway, and the eminences above Monmouth, bound the horizon. Above, and on the side of Brecknockshire, all was clear and bright; but below, and to the south, there was much vapour and mist, which obscured the prospect and prevented my seeing the distant Severn, and the hills in Somersetshire and Gloucestershire.

Archdeacon William Coxe 1801

At the western end of the summit, scramble over the rocks and head down the Llangenny Path. After about ½ mile, bear left and head down the ridge to meet a stone wall. Descend to a stream at the head of Cwm Gwenffrwd and then go up the other side to cross a junction of tracks and then meet the Llanwenarth Breast car park track. Go straight across and follow a broad path that traverses around the hillside above St. Mary's Vale.

The track passes over a stream trickling down into the valley below and after a few yards you ignore the narrow path to the left and continue along the broad path. Keep straight on at the next junction and on reaching a fence turn left beside it. Don't go over the stile but walk on with the fence on your right. Observe how the Sugar Loaf summit now gradually changes in shape — becoming more and more pointed.

Soon the track dips down to cross another stream and then continues around above the Cibi Valley. On reaching a junction of tracks, bear left along a slightly rising path which soon levels out and then descends to rejoin your outward route. This is now followed back to the car park.

ROUTE 9

LLWYN DU CIRCUIT (5 miles, 3 hours)

'It looks like a piked ridge from the opposite side of the Usk; sometimes appears in a globular shape, but at a distance, and particularly at the south-eastern side of the Skyrrid, assumes the form of a pyramid, and resembles the crater of a volcano. The cone is the highesr object in the vicinity, has nothing rugged or craggy, and is characterised by smoothness and beauty.'

Archdeacon William Coxe 1801

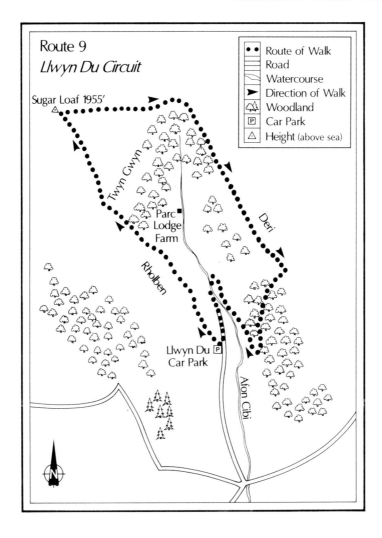

Start from Llwyn Du Car Park (SO 288166).

Go up the farm lane on the left leading up to Porth-y-Parc farm and continue through the farmyard. Soon ahead will be seen the conical summit of the Sugar Loaf.

Follow a broad lane between hedges to cross a stile. Then go on beside a fence and over another stile. The path becomes a sunken track ascending through the trees and provides pleasant views across the broad valley of Afon Cibi.

You then cross an open area and come to another stile. Just beyond this, where the track divides, keep left following the rising track and passing the remnants of a stone wall. Cross two stiles in rapid succession and then go through a gate.

At the next junction of tracks keep left and shortly afterwards look out for a rock on the left on which is cut an Ordnance Survey bench mark.

On reaching another stile, join the Rholben ridge track at Twyn Gwyn. Keep straight on for a short while and then turn right to follow a path leading directly up to the Sugar Loaf summit.

'During my continuance on the summit, I felt that extreme satisfaction which I always experience, when elevated on the highest point of the circumjacent country. The air is more pure, the body more active, and the mind more serene, lifted up above the dwellings of man, we discard all grovelling and earthly passions; the thoughts assume a character of sublimity proportionate to the grandeur of the surrounding objects, and as the body approaches nearer to the etherel regions, the soul imbibes a portion of their unalterable purity.'

Archdeacon Coxe

On leaving the summit, descend on the east side and follow a path down to the fence line above the Cibi valley. Turn left and follow a path beside the fence heading for the Deri ridge. At a division of tracks, keep right to eventually join the Deri ridge which is the easternmost of the three offshoots of the Sugar Loaf.

Now turn right and follow a broad path along the crest of the ridge, keeping right at the next junction. From here there are views of the Three Peaks. The bulky Blorenge is to the south, the jagged ridge of Skirrid Fawr to the east and the conical Sugar Loaf summit is now prominently behind you.

On reaching Allt (spot height 376m) at the end of the highest point of the Deri ridge, descend a short slope and at a track junction make a 90 degree turn to the right. At the next junction take the second track on the left and head down into the woods.

The track is carpeted with the long fallen leaves of countless autumns and it descends all the way with the Blorenge looming in the distance.

Go through a gate and opposite a bungalow on the other side, turn sharply right to pass through another gate. Then follow a broad track doubling back through the trees. It is a dog-leg section but provides very plesant walking with the Cibi heard tumbling down through the valley below. Go through another gate and the path narrows, following beside a fence to rise slightly and then drop down to join a farm lane. Turn left and head back to the starting point.

ROUTE 10

GLANGRWYNE CIRCUIT (6 miles, 3½ hours)

'The man who climbs merely to bag summits or to exercise his muscles misses too much. Mountain climbing can resemble wine-bibbing. To drink too much is to become satiated and uncaring; to drink good wine quickly and heedlessly is to drink with the damned. Therefore in mountaineering go slowly. Climb the lesser hills as well as the greater; their charms are not less.'

F.S. Smythe

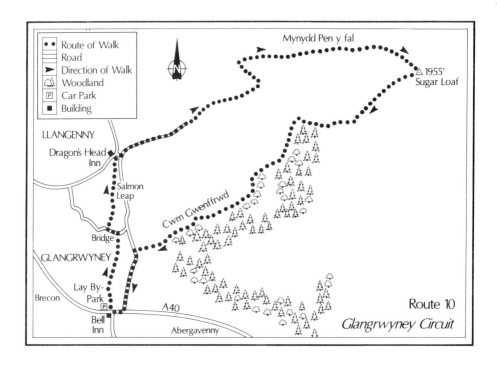

Park in a lay-by on the A40 in Glangrwyne next to a phone box. G.R. 231168. Almost opposite the Bell Hotel is a lane that runs beside the recreation field. This is followed for about 150 yards. Then cross a stile on the left and turn right to follow a path through a meadow. Go over another stile and continue through the next field beside the River Grwyne. Go over a stile at the end of the field and turn left along a road. After about 100 yards cross the river on a stone bridge and then go over a stile on the right, beneath an immense, gnarled and twisted walnut tree.

The Salmon Leap at Llangenny.   *Chris Barber*

Walk on beside the chattering river — cross a stile and continue through a field to reach another stile. Soon on your right you will pass the Llangenny Salmon Leap at the weir. Further on, you will also pass on your right, a stone building which was once a paper mill. Continue past the farmhouse and go through a gate.

To your left is a solitary standing stone which was placed in this field in pre-historic times and is known locally as the Druid Stone. At the end of the farm drive, turn right along a road to pass (or stop for a drink) at the Dragon's Head Inn which is situated in Llangenny.

This pretty little village takes its name from Cenau, a daughter of Brychan, one-time ruler of the ancient kingdom of Brycheiniog. St. Cenau founded a simple chuch here in the 6th century. Both the hamlets of Glangrwyne and Llangenny were renowned for their paper mills from the end of the eighteenth century up to 1938.

Turn right and cross the stone bridge arching over the River Grwyne Fechan. On the other side, turn left and follow the road past the gatehouse to Pen-y-Darren House (now an Outdoor Activity Centre) and continue steeply up beside a long stone wall.

On reaching a cross roads keep straight on past the white house and continue uphill until you reach the head of the valley where the road turns to the right in a hair-pin bend and becomes a private drive to Pentwyn.

49

Go straight on at the bend and through a gate, to follow a stony track leading up between a fence and the remains of a stone wall. Pass through another gate and the track now steepens slightly and heads up to a gate in a stone wall. Turn left along a broad sandy track, enjoying views up through the Usk Valley towards the Brecon Beacons. Ahead can be seen Table Mountain and the limestone capped peak of Pen Cerrig Calch.

The track takes you around a corner and past the site of an old quarry. Turn right now up a broad path following the crest of the ridge. It heads up through the heather over a series of humps. For a long time the summit of the Sugar Loaf is hidden from view but as you come over a rise the rocky crest of the summit appears on the skyline (unless its a misty day of course!). You are just 15-20 minutes from the summit now.

This last section of the ridge is like a switch- back for the path takes you over a series of humps. On the right is Cwm Gwenffrwd, down which the return journey is to be made. Scramble up through the rocks to gain the long flat summit. Touch the trig' point and take in the view.

View of Table Mountain and Pen Cerrig Calch.   *Chris Barber*

Just past the trig' point follow a diagonal path down to the right, heading down to the Llanwenarth ridge. Follow it down to a crossing of tracks and then turn right. Now descend steeply into Cwm Gwenffrwd, cross a stream and go up the other side to follow a path down the right hand side of the valley.

Go through a gate and keep straight on down to reach another gate. The path gently descends all the way now above a narrow wooded valley. Continue beside a fence and above a dingle to reach a stile beside a gate. On the opposite side of the valley is a lovely old farmhouse nestling in a sheltered hollow. The path soon joins a cart track which takes you down through a field, past a barn, through a gate and down a road to reach a T junction. Turn left here and follow the road down to the A40. Cross the road and follow the pavement back to your starting point.

ABERGAVENNY, 'THE GATEWAY TO WALES'

Most people who have written about Abergavenny seem to agree that it is situated in a well chosen spot. The earliest mention of it as a place must surely be the one provided by the Roman historian Tacitus who tells us that Gobannium was a military station mid-way between Isca (Caerleon) and Y Gaer (Brecon) on the road north to Deva (Chester).

John Leland the 16th century antiquarian found the country around Abergavenny, *'sumwat mountayneous.'* He described the place as a *'faire walled town, neatly inhabited.'*

Another author writing in 1602 was even more convinced of Abergavenny's attributes for he remarked that it *'was a fine town, wealthy and thriving and the very best in the Shire.'*

John Wesley, the founder of the Methodist Movement, first visited Abergavenny in 1739 and in his journal he recorded that he returned on *'Saturday 3rd October, 1741. We had a plain useful sermon on the Pharisee and the Publican praying in the Temple which I explained at large in the evening to the best-dressed congregation I have ever yet seen in Wales.'*

My namesake J.T. Barber who came here in 1803, was impressed by the surrounding hills. He observed that:-
*'On approaching Abergavenny, the tourist's attention is involuntarily arrested by the singular beauty and variety of interest which the spot embraces, particularly in its encircling hills. The road skirting the Little Skyridd, a well formed hill richly laid out in wood and pasture, opens to a fine display of the Vale of Usk beneath; on the opposite side of which the continuous ridge of the wild Pontypool hills, which form the western boundary of the county, terminate in the heathy high-swelling Blorenge; a tract of wood sweeps along its base, and mixes with the sylvan knoll of Llanfoist, decorating its northern extremity. Further to the right, the elegant smooth cone of the Sugar Loaf, the highest of the Monmouthshire mountains presents itself, issuing from among the four tributary eminences of the Pen-y-Val hills. Eastward of the mountain is the Great Skyrrid, an object of considerable interest; its bipartite and truly Alpine summit, without being a forced opposition, strikingly contrasts with the general undulating line of the neighbouring hills, and rears a distinct and noble character to the scene. The views from this mountain are scarcely inferior to those from the Sugar Loaf; while its craggy form, its asperitous summit, jagged into an immense fissure, and shelving to ridge apex of fearful narrowness, impress a mixed emotion of awe and admiration on the adventurous climber of the height, that more than compensates for a small inferiority of altitude.
'The expansive bases of these mountains nearly approximately descend to a finely-wooded fertile valley, through which the River Usk, rushing from a majestic portal of wood, winds in a bright translucid stream, with all the impetuosity of its*

mountain character. At the foot of one of the confederated hills, sustaining the lowering cone of the Sugar-Loaf, which gently inclines to the river, Abergavenny is situated; a straggling irregular town, pleasantly-interspersed with trees, but deriving its highest attraction from the charm of its position.'

Old tramroad bridge across the River Usk.   *19th Century Engraving*

Wirt Sikes, The United States Consul to Wales in 1879, also emphasised that: *'The special charm of Abergavenny town is its situation at the base of and surrounded by mountains, and shadowed in the near distance by the russet peak called Mynydd Pen-y-Fal, about 2,000 feet high.*

'A clean, quaint collection of stone houses is Abergavenny, with half a dozen comely churches and chapels, and a ruined castle. Modern map-makers have had the effrontery to tell us that Abergavenny is not in Wales, but in England - a statement which would be disproved, one would suppose, by the Welsh name of the town, its Welsh customs, Welsh history, and Welsh people; but if any obstinate person should side with the aforesaid map-makers in spite of these, let him be crushed by an invitation to a concert at the Cymmreigyddion Hall, in Tudor Street, Abergavenny. It must be a bold spirit which would call Cymreigyddion Hall an English place of entertainment.'

John White writing in 1877 provides a convincing answer to the question of whether Monmouthshire was in England or Wales:

'Monmouthshire was by an act of Henry VII nominally added to the English counties to be included in the circuits of the English judges, nevertheless it virtually remained as much a part of Wales as before, and continued to be included as such

in most of the tourist's accounts and Histories of the Principality. The Welsh in speaking of the extent of the Principality always said "Y Tair Sir arddeg o Cymry," - "the thirteen counties of Wales".'

It is fascinating to read the different impressions that people have of a place that are very often gained from one or two brief visits when the weather is perhaps a little unusual. In 1905 Charles Harper observed that, *'When it is a period of sunshine, Abergavenny Castle basks in a mellow heat; when the mists gather and disperse in those hours of rain and vapours, the townsmen, if they have souls for such things are free of a beautiful effect; and when storms of thunder and lightning break over those lovely summits and go reverberating from end to end of the vale, like the tattoo of some infernal drummer, then the town commands a spectacle of theatric grandeur.'*

A.G. Bradley observed that Abergavenny *'like most border towns that sprung from a Norman castle, and for obvious reasons, its streets are on a slope. It is now an English and not a Welsh town both in habit and appearance, boasting a mayor and corporation, ten thousand people, golf links, cricket ground, and a famous salmon river. It is on the main line for Bristol, London or the north, has a marquis close at hand and a select and wealthy neighbourhood, so it should be happy. It manufactures nothing notable, I believe, but has a railroad which climbs the mountains across the Usk and taps the mining country which lies for the most part so mercifully hidden behind them and should bring trade and traffic. In short, Abergavenny is in itself a pleasant average country town, neither remarkable nor the reverse in its construction.'*

John White, who wrote a guidebook to the town and its neighbourhood in 1877 sums up the situation of Abergavenny in a very convincing manner and was obviously very fond of the place:-
'The Usk is seen winding its silvery course between banks lined with tall and luxuriant trees. Behind all this, the eye discovers an immense mass of mountains darkening the horizon. Immediately westwards is seen the broad-breasted Blorenge (Blawreng) scowling upon the plain beneath and towering magnificently and proudly. To the right we find the Little Scyrryd which presents a humble contrast to the grand character of the rest of the landscape. If this glorious assemblage of nature's charms does not rivet the eye of the traveller as it bursts upon his view, he may be put down as devoid of all feeling for the beautiful and sublime.'

But I will leave the last word to Edward J. Burrow who in 1903 summed up in one sentence the feelings that many local people have with regard to Abergavenny as a place of importance:-
'When country folk come in to do their week's shopping, all is different; there is a long row of vehicles all up the main street, and the pavement is thronged with farmers and their women folk, to each of whom Abergavenny is the hub of the world.'

ROUTE 11

THE MASSACRE WALK (9 miles, allow 5 hours)

This walk has been included in order to tell the story of a famous and grue-some event that took place in Abergavenny during the latter part of the twelfth century. It would be appropriate to walk the route on Christmas Day pausing for an outdoor banquet on the way, but watch out for the ghosts of the murdered Welshmen and the wicked William de Braose, a Norman baron who was known as the 'Ogre of Abergavenny'!

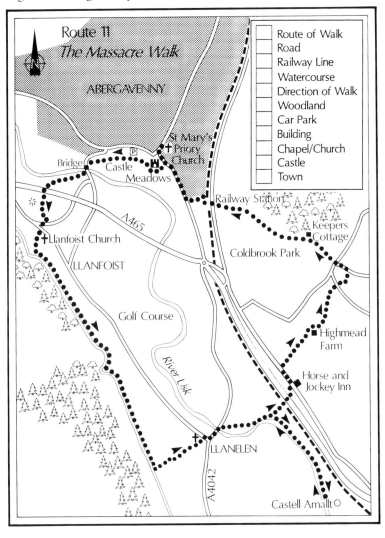

St. Mary's Priory Church.   *Albert Lyons Collection*

An appropriate starting point for this walk is St. Mary's Priory Church beside the Hereford Road. It is a large cruciform building with a central battlemented tower, choir and transepts. Formerly it was a chapel to the old Benedictine Priory with the chancel forming the monastic church while the nave served as the parish church. Hamelyn de Balon established the priory in about 1090 and endowed it to support a prior and twelve monks. It was attached as a cell to the abbey of St. Vincent near Le Mans.

In 1408 the priory was badly damaged when Owain Glyndwr reputedly set fire to Abergavenny and when it was dissolved in 1543 there were only four monks and a prior still living there, while its revenues were worth a mere £59 4s per annum.

From that time the priory church became the parish church of St. Mary and today there are few signs of the Benedictine priory that once stood here. The original stone altar was discovered many years ago built into the interior wall of an Abergavenny inn. It was removed and taken to Holy Trinity Church in Baker Street.

A Victorian writer once described St. Mary's as the 'Westminster Abbey of South Wales', so impressed was he with its fine monuments, tombs and mural tablets. They are undoubtedly a fascinating collection of memorials to the Marcher barons and some of the important families who once lived in this part of Gwent.

Close to the altar can be seen these monuments to some of the Norman barons and knights who once rode with heads held high through the streets of Abergavenny. They lie here, in effigy, crosslegged, with hands pressed together in prayer while beneath their helmets their vacant eyes gaze towards the roof of the church. The monuments are in fact older than the existing church for it was mainly rebuilt in the 14th century.

Visitors are always impressed by the size of the church for it is 172 feet long and five arches separate the nave from the north aisle. They appear light and graceful when compared to the solid masonry of the tower arches, which are adorned with ballflower ornament and sculptured heads.

The choir-stalls are a legacy from medieval times and there are twenty-four of them carved in oak. They end with the stalls of the prior and sub-prior set under lofty pinnacles decorated with fine open tracery on their four sides. One stall bears the name of William of Winchester, a prior in 1493.

In the nave is a stained glass window illustrating the Acts of the Apostles. It also shows scenes from St. Paul's Conversion and the figures of six other saints.

A mural tablet on the south wall of the Nave commemorates a popular local surgeon who once lived in the town.

In memory of William Steel, for 55 years
a resident in this town, Died Nov. 11th,
1861. 'A Surgeon, kind, skilful, and
courageous.'

Other members of this family who were also doctors and surgeons are buried in the churchyard at Llanfoist and their memorial stones may be inspected on Walk 3.

The Norman font-bowl adorned with cable ornament lay buried in the churchyard for two centuries and was unearthed in 1897.

A very fine wooden effigy in the nave probably represents George de Cantelupe, 10th Lord of Abergavenny who died in 1273 aged twenty. There are only about one hundred such monuments in the churches of Britain and this particular effigy is considered to be one of the finest.

In the floor of the nave is a sepulchral stone in the floor which bears an interesting epitaph:-

Here lieth one of Abel's race,
Whom Cain did hunt from place to place;
Yet, not dismayed, about he went,
Working until his days were spent.
Now, having done, he takes a nap
Here in our common mother's lap
Waiting to hear the Bridegroom say
'Arise, my dear, and come away.'

Obiit. Hen Maurice. 30 die, Solii 1612

The east window of the sanctuary is particularly fine and worth more than a casual glance. In the centre can be seen the Madonna sitting in a throne with the infant Jesus standing on her lap. On one side is St. Christopher, walking out of a stream with young Jesus on his shoulder. St. Michael stands with his scales on the other side and portrayed in the outer lights are the Saints Luke and Mark. Below is a Crucifixion scene, with the cross formed from the foliage of a lily and small figures of angels, saints and martyrs can be seen in the tracery.

Flanking the sanctuary are two chapels which contain some fascinating treasures. On the north side is the Lewis Chapel which takes its name from the 16th century monument of Dr. David Lewis, the first Principal of Jesus College, Oxford and Judge of the High Court of Admiralty in the reign of Elizabeth I. He was born in Abergavenny and was the son of the Rev. Lewis Wallis, Vicar of Abergavenny and Llantilio Pertholey. He was buried here on May 24th 1854.

An effigy of a woman bearing a shield on her breast is said to be Eva de Cantelupe who became Baroness of Abergavenny in 1257. It depicts her lying on a stone slab with her head resting on an oblong cushion and with a dog at her feet. Covering the body is a large shield bearing the arms of the Cantelupe family. This is unusual for generally only knights were carved with their shields. She was the daughter of Eva de Braose and her husband was William de Cantelupe who died in 1256. Eva died the following year. Her infant son and heir was George de Cantelupe.

Nearby is the effigy of Eva de Braose who died in 1246. She was the daughter of William Marshall, Earl of Pembroke and her husband William de Braose, Lord of Abergavenny was a grandson of an earlier William de Braose who was known as the 'Ogre of Abergavenny'.

On Eva's figure is said to be part of the image of a squirrel. There is a popular story that recalls how she kept the furry creature as a pet. One day while she was walking in the grounds of Abergavenny Castle, it ran from her. She followed it to the top of a wall and overbalanced to fall to her death.

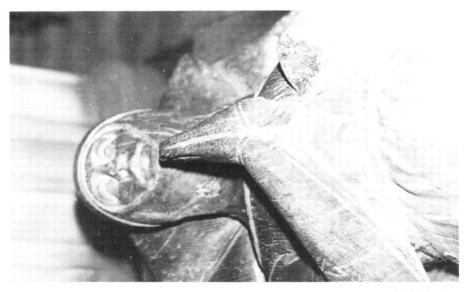

Wooden effigy of George de Cantelupe.   *Chris Barber*

Having described these first three monuments it is only fair to add that in recent years doubts have been cast upon their identities. It is now thought that the wooden effigy long thought to be George de Cantelupe the 10th Lord of Abergavenny may possibly represent John de Hastings. The one identifed as Eva de

Cantelupe is now believed to be a monument to her daughter Joan de Hastings who married Henry de Hastings. When her brother George died the barony of Abergavenny passed to her and then to her son John de Hastings. It would seem that only her heart is buried in Abergavenny for Joan was buried with her husband in the church of The Friars Minor on the outskirts of Coventry. Doubt has also be cast upon the identity of the effigy of Eva de Braose which is currently thought to be that of Margaret Windsor, sister of the Black Prince and daughter of Edward III.

Tomb of Sir Richard Herbert of Ewyas.   *Bill Barber*

On the south side of the Lewis Chapel in a canopied recess is an effigy of Sir Richard Herbert of Ewyas who died in 1510.

The Herbert Chapel on the south side of the sanctuary contains some of the finest monumental tombs in Britain and they reflect the long history of Norman rule and oppression of this area. Here the Norman lords of Abergavenny lie beside some equally famous Welshmen. It is the last resting place of the Herberts of Coldbrook, once a large estate just outside Abergavenny, which later became the home of Charles Hanbury Williams.

Sir Richard Herbert of Coldbrook is represented in a full suit of mail, with his head supported by a sheaf of arrows, which was his crest. His feet are resting on a lion which is significant, for he was a tall and strong man who was renowned for his feats of strength. The heroism that he displayed in 1459 at the battle of Banbury was vividly described by his descendant Lord Herbert of Cherbury. *'With his pole-axe he passed and re-passed twice through the enemy's army and killed with his own hand 140 men.'* But when his force were on the point of gaining an impressive victory, the Welsh troops mistook a small corps of the army for the advanced guard of the Lancastrian party, under the Earl of Warwick. They panicked and fled on all sides while Sir Richard Herbert and his brother the Earl of Pembroke bravely remained on the field of battle. They were taken prisoners and led in triumph to Banbury, where they were sentenced to death the following day. The Earl of Pembroke was subsequently buried in Tintern Abbey.

Beside brave Sir Richard Herbert lies the effigy of his wife, who wears a long robe; her head rests on a cushion, supported by two angels which unfortunately have been mutilated, and her feet rest on two dogs. It is doubtful whether this effigy is a true life-size representation, because if it is, then she would have been a very tall woman, for it is the same length and bulk as that of her husband, measuring 6 feet 4 inches in length!

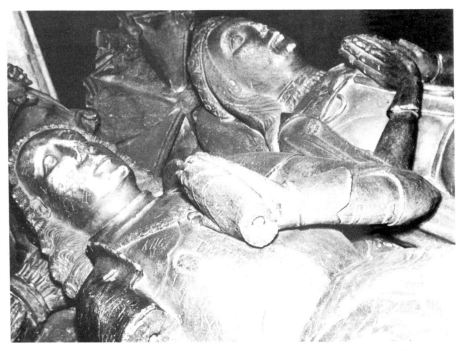

Sir Richard Herbert of Coldbrook and his wife.   *Chris Barber*

59

The Jesse Tree.   *Chris Barber*

In the west end of the chapel is a massive figure carved out of a single piece of oak. It is ten feet long and has large beard and dishevelled hair. At one time it was believed to represent St. Christopher, carrying, according to legend, the child Jesus across a river. However, it was later realised that it is in fact the remains of a Jesse tree and probably the finest in existence. It depicts Jesse asleep reclining on his left side; his head covered with a cap and he reposes on a cushion supported by an angel. From the left side of his body grows the stem of a tree which is held or supported by the left hand of the figure, just above the tree which has been sawn off.

It is a representation of the genealogy of Christ, from David, formed by a tree growing out of the body of Jesse, the father of David. Originally the tree would have been complete with branches where statuettes would have been positioned among the foliage to represent the various persons from whom he was descended. The highest statue of all would have been a representation of the Saviour. Churchyard, who came here in 1587 described it as 'a most famous worke in manner of a genealogy of kings, called the Roote of Jesse, which work is defaced and pulled down in pieces'.

Jesse Trees were occasionally made to form the Reredos of an Altar and this one may have formed part of the Screen between the Choir and the Lady Chapel which used to occupy the present Chancel. When complete it must have looked magnificent and what remains is a fine example of 15th century carving or perhaps even earlier. The figure was probably pulled down at the time of the Re-

60

formation and the bulk of it used for firewood. The culprits were probably Colonel Fairfax and his Roundheads who tore down and burned most of the furnishings and antique woodwork in this church.

Apparently the figure was placed in its present position in 1828 and it rests on a bed of stone, the front of which is from an altar-tomb. Other remnants of Jesse Trees can be seen in St. Cuthbert's Church, Wells, and at Christchurch in Hampshire but the Abergavenny one is by far the finest.

Sir Edward Neville, carved in stone as a knight clad in armour reclines with a bull at his feet. This seems a strange animal for him to rest his feet on and a rather dubious story is sometimes related as an explanation. It is said that this very strong man once seized a bull by its horns and broke them off, whereupon the bull ran away roaring with pain. Sir Edward Neville became Baron of Abergavenny after marrying Elizabeth, daughter of Richard de Beauchamp.

However, doubt has recently been cast upon the identification of this effigy, for it has been suggested that it in fact represents Lawrence de Hastings a Lord of Abergavenny who died on 13th August 1348 and was buried here in the Priory Church. The crest of the Hastings family was a bull's head which certainly seems significant.

An alabaster figure of Sir William ap Thomas also clad in armour lies with his wife Gladys who was a daughter of Sir David Gam who fought alongside Henry V at the battle of Agincourt. During the battle, he helped to save the life of his king but in doing so received terrible wounds. He was knighted by Henry as he lay dying on the field of battle. His wife Gladys was so poular that when she died, a procession of 3,000 knights, noblemen and peasants followed her funeral from Coldbrooke to St. Mary's Church.

Sadly these magnificent monuments, once plastered with white lime have been disfigured by numerous initials and names, many of them cut by mischievious boys, when the Herbert Chapel was used as a schoolroom in the 19th century.

It is time that we started our walk.

Outside the church, turn left beside the massive stone barn. The nesting holes in the wall of the barn facing the church car park would have been for doves. They would have supplied the Gunter family who lived in the priory during the 18th century with eggs and no doubt dove pie was frequently on the menu as well.

Follow the lane down to a car park, which occupies the site of the old priory ponds. Also on this side of the church used to stand the old Priory House, which was once the living headquarters of the Benedictine monks. When the priory was dissolved, the possessions of the estate were granted to James Gunter of Breconshire. He developed the house into a mansion which remained in his family until the beginning of the eighteenth century. Both Charles I and Charles II are said to have stayed there and one room was known as the King's Bedroom.

Turn right and go past the public toilets (it is always useful to know where they are !), to reach the main road and walk down Mill Street passing Tan House on your left. A plaque on the wall informs you that this was once the 'centre of a thriving tanning industry until 1884.'

Above now to the right you will hardly fail to observe the walls of Abergavenny Castle with its square sham keep perched on top of the old Norman motte. It was built in 1818 by the Marquis of Abergavenny whose main home at that time was Eridge Castle in Kent. His Abergavenny estate steward supervised the construction of this building which took two years to complete and was known as 'The Court House'. The Nevill family made use of it for a few years as a shooting box and then leased it as a private house.

Abergavenny Castle.   *Albert Lyons Collection*

Cross the road and ascend a flight of stone steps to follow a tarmac path around the external wall of the castle. From here the views across the Usk Valley towards the Blorenge and up river to Llanfoist Bridge and the distant limestone hills of Mynydd Llangattock are particularly pleasing. Follow the wall around to reach the castle entrance.

The first castle at Abergavenny was built by Hamelin de Ballon, the son of Drogo de Baladon, who came from Maine in Normandy with William the Conqueror. He was assigned the conquest of Over Gwent and as there is no account of any battle having taken place, it is probable that he achieved his purpose with little resistance. It was William the Conqueror's son William Rufus who gave Hamelin the title Lord of Abergavenny.

In about 1090 he consolidated his position by erecting a timber tower on top of an artificial mound and surrounded it with a wooden stockade. After residing here for nearly twenty years this Norman knight died without issue. He was buried in St. Mary's Priory which he also founded. The lordship of Monmouth he left to his nephew Withenock, son of his brother William, and the lordship of Abergavenny to his nephew Brian de Wallingford. This Norman knight is supposed to have built a hospital somewhere near Yspitty Farm on the outskirts of the town, where he placed his two leper sons. Also he granted large endowments to the priory on behalf of his unfortunate youngsters.

De Wallingford is notorious for having plundered the Cathedral of Llandaff and to atone for his wrong doings he travelled to the Holy Land, giving the Lordship of Abergavenny to the son of his first cousin, Walter the son of Miles, Earl of Hereford. He made his mark by replacing the timber tower with a stone keep and the stockade with a substantial curtain wall.

In 1128 the castle was held by Brian de Insula, but his sons did not succeed, as both of them also had the misfortune to be lepers. So the castle and its lands passed to Milo, Constable of England and Earl of Hereford. He was accidently killed in 1144 while hunting. His five sons had all died childless so the extensive estates of the family were divided among the three daughters. The Abergavenny estate was inherited by Beta, the wife of Phillip de Braose. They had a son named William who in later years was to become known as the 'Ogre of Abergavenny'.

Walking past Abergavenny Castle.   *Chris Barber*

Today, all that remains of the 12th century fortress are the gatehouse, the masonry of two towers and the connecting outer walls to the foundations of the keep which stood on a mound which had been formed on a terminal moraine. It is of interest that the River Usk has changed its course, for it once flowed closer to the motte. The lodge at the entrance to the castle was built in Victorian times and it stands near the site of a defensive ditch and drawbridge.

As you pass through the broken archway of the massive gatehouse try to imagine a party of about seventy Welshmen arriving here on Christmas Day in 1177.

Arrival of the Welshmen at Abergavenny Castle 1177.   *Sally Davies*

Their leader was Sitsyllt ap Dyfnawl the local Welsh Prince and they had been by William de Braose to attend a banquet. Not suspecting his motives, they came willingly and on their arrival were treated with warm hospitality.

Banquet scene in the Great Hall, Abergavenny Castle.   *Sally Davies*

Sitsyllt was no stranger to this castle, for early one morning in 1172, he and his men had managed to force their way inside, just as the guard was being withdrawn. They captured the constable, his family and most of the soldiers. During the attack, Henry Fitz-Milo 4th Lord of Abergavenny was killed. He was the uncle of William de Braose and the last of the Hamelin line. Abergavenny Castle then remained in Sitsyllt's possession until 1175, when he was persuaded by his brother-in-law Rhys ap Gruffyd, a staunch ally of King Henry II to surrender it to the Norman Lordship. Soon afterwards Sitsyllt was summoned by the king to attend his court at Gloucester. It was a royal gathering of Welsh princes and even included those who had committed violent acts. Undoubtedly this was a day of goodwill, when crimes were forgotten and bonds of trust and friendship were forged. Sitsyllt was one of many Welshmen to be granted the king's pardon that day, in return for his voluntary withdrawl from Abergavenny Castle.

It was soon afterwards, following his return to Gwent, that Sitsyllt and other local Welsh noblemen received the invitation from William de Braose, the new Lord of Abergavenny to gather at his castle for a celebration of the reconciliation at a grand banquet.

On taking up his inheritance, William de Braose became the 5th Lord of Abergavenny and he took up residence in the castle with his wife Maud St. Valerie. She is sometimes referred to as Maud Wallbee and it has been said that she was as powerful and grasping as her evil husband. Her dowry included Brecknock and Hay and it was not long before the Lordship of Abergavenny became the most powerful in Wales.

65

When the band of Welshmen arrived for the banquet, they were politely asked to leave their weapons in the gatehouse and they duly complied.

We pass through the ruined archway and shortly on the right can be seen the site of the Great Hall where the banquet was held. In its heyday this immense hall measured 92 feet by 54 feet but now only a portion of its south and west walls, with traces of a spiral stone staircase can be seen.

The guests sat down at long tables loaded with food and William de Braose rose to his feet and welcomed the Welshmen to Abergavenny Castle. But after the goblets had been passed around, he changed the tone of his voice and announced that henceforth all the Welsh of his domain should be deprived of the right to carry arms, and that all who were present should swear to abandon that right. His guests were deeply shocked by his words and no doubt stared at him in astonishment, for they had come here that night in good faith and had not expected such a demand.

Massacre of the Welshmen by the Norman soldiers.   *Sally Davies*

Then de Braose gave a pre-arranged signal and soldiers led by Ranulph Poer, the Sheriff of Hereford rushed into the hall with gleaming swords in their hands. The Welshmen now rose to their feet in horror. Without their weapons they were unable to defend themselves and they were savagely cut to pieces. Their blood mingled with the wine that they had been drinking and one by one they fell to the stone floor until the massacre was complete. It is reputed however that Prince Iorwerth of Caerleon managed to escape. It is said that he managed to procure a Norman's sword and hewing his way to the door, he escaped into the blackness of the December night.

Not satisfied with this bloodshed, William de Braose, the next morning ordered his men to saddle their horses and they rode down the Usk Valley to Sitsyllt's home at Castell Arnallt. The Welshman's widow was forced to stand helpless as her infant son Cadwaladr was slain before her very eyes.

With these grim pictures in your mind, leave the castle, turn left and shortly walk down a path to reach the Cycleway Route which is at present used more by walkers than cyclists. It snakes across Castle Meadows and brings you to Llanfoist Bridge.

Castle Meadows was once a part of the Lordship lands and passed to the Nevill family in 1445. In Coxe's 'Tours in Monmouthshire,' published in 1801, a map shows the meadows divided into smaller fields by hedges, while today it is of course one large field. At one time these water-meadows were used by the Welsh drovers as a pound for cattle that they had driven here from the mountains of Mid Wales. In the 1870's the meadows began to have a recreational use, for the Abergavenny Cricket Club played here. The Nevill family owned this land until 1916, when William Nevill the 1st Marquis of Abergavenny died and the Monmouthshire estates were sold.

Turn left and cross Llanfoist Bridge which used to be known as Tudor Bridge after Jasper Tudor the uncle of Henry VII. He was at one time Lord of Abergavenny and caused the bridge to be built. Originally it had sixteen arches but when it was rebuilt at a later date the number of arches was reduced to eight.

A field above the bridge used to be known as Cae'r Bed — the 'Field of the Grave.' An old book on the area recalls that when the dreaded plague came to Abergavenny, the bodies of those who died from it were *conveyed in waggons and buried here in their clothes just as they appeared when death came on the scene, in large pits dug for that purpose, and about the same time as that of the Great Plague in London.*

At the end of the bridge, cross the road and follow the lane leading past the cemetery. It turns a corner and then drops down to pass beneath the Heads of the Valleys Road. As you pass the market garden, look to the right to see a large mound partly obscured by trees. Not far away is the site of the battle of 'Cad Ivor' which was fought in the Dark Ages and the mound allegedly covers the bodies of those who were slain. This local story is not necessarily true, but it certainly provides a reason for the mound. It is practically circular and about 70 yards in diameter. Near the top, a pit was once dug, presumably by an optimistic treasure hunter.

On reaching the main road, go straight across. Near here used to stand Llanfoist Brewery and within a few hundred yards of it there were once three public houses, but the Llanfoist Inn is the only one that remains. The others were Waterloo House and the New Inn which is now a post office.

Carry on up the lane past Llanfoist Church to reach a tunnel passing beneath the canal. Don't go through it but ascend the steps on the right to reach the tranquil and picturesque Llanfoist Wharf (described in Route 4). Turn left here and follow the towpath under a low bridge. Views can now be enjoyed over Abergavenny towards the two Skirrids. See if you can pick out the green topped tower of the Town Hall, the tower of St. Mary's Church and Abergavenny Castle.

Below to the left can be seen Lower Llanfoist Farm where Abergavenny Race Course was once situated. The manor of Lower Llanfoist was retained by the descendants of Ynyr King of Gwent after the arrival of the Normans. It was here that Garwyn ap Caradawg the uncle of Sitsyllt ap Dwynfal lived. From those distant times right up until the middle of the 18th century, his descendants, who latterly adopted the surname of Price remained at Llanfoist, occupying a leading position among the gentry of the county.

The towpath takes you past a little canal-side cottage and beneath a stone bridge. Then after another mile, pass beneath another stone bridge and go around a bend to glimpse a wooded ravine through which a stream passing beneath the canal flows. Further on, pass under another stone bridge and within a mile you will reach a bridge that spans the canal with the sole purpose of providing access to fields on either side. Go over a stile beside this bridge and head down through a field to cross a stile in the bottom right-hand corner.

Head down through the small 'executive style' housing estate to reach Llanelen Church. Pause here to examine the grave of Sir Thomas Phillips. It is the one in the corner of the graveyard that is surrounded by iron railings. He used to own a country house in Llanelen and is best remembered for his connections with Newport. At the time of the Chartists' riots in 1839, he was Mayor of the town and received a knighthood for his courage in standing up to the rioters, despite being wounded in the arm by a musket ball.

The Parish Church of St. Helen has been rebuilt in the Gothic style and consequently is now of little interest apart from an unusual sundial, which was once built into the churchyard wall. It is now inside the church and resembles the bowl of a font in which are carved rays and an iron pointer.

Roman coins were found near Llanelen in 1961 when Mr. Edward Jones was excavating a potato field on Ty Aur Farm. He noticed something gleaming and bent down to pick up a gold piece of the Emperor Claudius (41-54). Ty Aur of course means 'House of Gold' and a barn in an adjoining field bears the equally intriguing name of Ysgubor Aur — 'Gold Barn'. This suggests that perhaps sometime in the past a hoard of gold was discovered here.

On the right is Llanelen Post Office which was once the Hanbury Inn. Lady Llanover who succeeded in closing down several pubs in this locality, converted it into a temperance house and re-named it Y Seren Gobaith — 'The Star of Hope.' Apparently the main road (A4042) passes over the cellars of the old inn. Lady Llanover also closed down the Red Lion which was the other pub in this village but the locals no doubt made use of the three pubs in Llanfoist instead.

An inscription on the south parapet of Llanelen Bridge states that it was *'Designed and built by John Upton of Gloucester, Engineer 1821 for the County of Monmouth.'* In later years he went bankrupt and fled to Russia where he was given the responsibility of planning the fortifications of Sebastopol, immediately prior to the Crimea War.

Keeping close to the side of the bridge, cross to the other side and go over a stile on the right. Turn left beside a fence and walk across a field. Then cross a ditch and a stile. Now continue along the path beside the Usk; go over two more stiles in quick succession and follow the fence, now looking down on the river. Cross a stile beside a gate (Remember this stile as a marker on the return journey) and follow the path around the edge of the next two fields to reach a prominent oak tree. Here the waymarked path descends to river level.

Cross a stile and walk a plank over a stream. The path continues beside the river and soon reaches a point where the bank is covered with flood debris deposited by the Usk when swollen by heavy rain. Pick your way through a mass of boughs and branches and ponder on the amazing power of water.

In due course you will notice on the left a substantial stone barn. To the right of it is an oblong grass covered mound. This is the site of Castell Arnallt. Its history is somewhat vague but according to legend the ancient name of this site is connected with Arnallt (or Ernault) the son of Bwch, who is supposed to have built the first fortress here. There is no way of confirming this, but the site was certainly occupied by the Welsh Prince Sitsyllt in the 12th century. It would have been a very basic sort of fortress consisting of a collection of wooden huts surrounded by a wooden stockade. From this base Sitsyllt and his officials would have administered the area under their control. He was the last of the kings of Over Gwent who had any authority in the district and strongly opposed to the Norman invasion, he was constantly at war with his enemies.

When William de Braose's men came here to murder Sitsyllt's infant son they set fire to the wooden fortress and took the grief stricken widow, Anharad back to Abergavenny Castle, where she no doubt died in the castle dungeons.

Site of Castell Arnallt, once the home of Sitsyllt ap Dyfnawl.   *Chris Barber*

The site of Castell Arnallt was then taken over by the Normans as a manor of the Lords of Abergavenny. There is a record that in 1349 it was in the possession of John Wallis, who was also known as Gallis. He paid rent for the land to Lawrence de Hastings, the 13th Lord of Abergavenny, but it is most unlikely that an inhabited residence stood here after 1177, so Wallis probably used the estate purely for agricultural purposes.

Sitsyllt's descendants continued to live in the neighbourhood and from Aeddan, his eldest son, came the families of Arnold of Llanfihangel Crucorney, Probert of Pant Glas, Reynolds of Llantrissant and Morgan of Llanwenarth. One of Sitsyllt's uncles was Garwyn and descended from him were the Prices of Llanfoist. The name Sitsyllt has undergone various alterations including Sytylt, Sissillt, Seycil or Seisel and ultimately Cecil. Robert Cecil was from this family and he became a highly-regarded counsellor to Queen Elizabeth I.

Retrace your steps along the waymarked path beside the river and on reaching the stile previously mentioned as a 'marker for the return journey', after crossing it turn right and walk beside the fence and a line of recently planted trees (protected by box fences). On reaching the corner of the field go over two stiles in quick succession, where a small plot of land has been fenced and planted with trees. Now turn left along a surfaced lane that runs parallel with the railway. Go through a gate and turn right to follow the road beneath the railway and the A40. It leads up to the old road to Raglan.

Cross the road opposite the Horse and Jockey Inn and go left along the pavement. Just past the house and barn on the right ('Speedwell'), go through a gate and walk up a rutted track through a field. Then go through a gate and continue up the next field to reach another gate. From here the track curves around to the right following the drive of Highmead Farm. Opposite the corner of a barn go left and through the right of two gates, to follow a broad rutted track up the next field with a stream now coming down on the right. At the top of the field go through the left hand of two gates and follow the hedge on your right. As you come over a rise a splendid view of Blorenge, Sugar Loaf and Skirrid Fach will appear.

Go over a stile in the top right-hand corner of the field and turn left along a road. On reaching a junction turn right. You are now looking down into Coldbrook Park. Continue past a road on the right (to Llandewi Rhydderch) and then shortly go through a gate on the left. Walk on beside a fence to follow a cart track along the edge of the next field. Pass through another gate and around the edge of another field. Then go through another gate and around the edge of the next field, passing beneath pylon cables.

Just below a secluded dwelling known as 'Keeper's Cottage', go over a stile beside a gate and then shortly cross a cart track. Ascend a few steps and go over a stile. Follow the left edge of the next field with an ancient hollow lane on the left, and walk on beside the domineering pylons.

Down to the left now can be seen the old stable block of the Coldbrook Estate. This used to be the principal mansion and estate in the parish and it takes its name from the brook flowing nearby. During the reign of Henry IV it was the seat of Sir Richard Herbert, but how he acquired it is not evident.

Sir Richard Herbert was the second son of Sir William ap Thomas of Raglan and brother of William, first Earl of Pembroke. Earlier on we saw his effigy in St. Mary's Priory Church. His widowed mother, Gwladys, the daughter of the famous Sir David Gam, also resided here at Coldbrook. She died in 1454 and was buried with her husband, Sir William ap Thomas, in the Priory Church.

On account of his stature Sir Richard Herbert was called Richard Hir (the tall). He was a brave soldier who fought under the White Rose in the Wars of the Roses. He married Margaret, a daughter of Thomas ap Gruffyd and sister to Sir Rhys ap Thomas who helped to place Henry VII on the throne.

In the 18th century the estate was bought by Major Hanbury of Pontypool for his son, Charles, who had a talent for writing poetry. He specialised in witty observations and political satire, but eventually became insane and died in 1759 at the age of fifty.

There are many fascinating stories connected with Coldbrook House, including the inevitable claim of an underground passage leading to Abergavenny Castle and some floor boards stained with a pool of blood during a sword fight on the stairs.

Lady Llanover purchased the estate in 1891 and today it is still owned by the Herbert family as a part of Llanover Estate. Coldbrook House at that time was a square building with a tower at each corner and from each side of the house ran an avenue of trees. On its southern side was a large deer park. Sadly the house was demolished in 1954.

Leaving the pylons behind you, the path descends to cross a stream trickling down into a dingle. Go over a stile and Abergavenny is now spread out below. Cross another stile and continue through the next field. Directly ahead now can be seen the tower of the Priory Church, the Town Hall clock tower and the Sugar Loaf rising proudly above the town.

The sloping field above you was once the site of a battle which occurred during the Norman Conquest, when Meuric was King of Gwent. A fierce dispute arose between the lesser rulers of Upper and Lower Gwent, and after several minor skirmishes the two bands of warriors met here for a final battle. The event is recorded in the 'Chronicle of the Kings, Lords and Chieftains of Wales', written and preserved at Bangor. This ancient manuscript tells us that the leader of the forces of Upper Gwent was killed, but, 'in spite of the death of their leader, the greater part of his followers returned to Abergavenny which was defended by a wall built by the Romans but now sadly destroyed.'

Follow the track down to the left and go over a stile. Cross a footbridge spanning a dingle and follow the path down through the next field to reach another stile. Cross the A465 and descend the bank on the other side to follow a path beside the fence adjoining the railway line. Go over the footbridge to reach Abergavenny Station.

Turn left along the pavement and make your way past the Great Western Hotel. On reaching the main road follow the pavement back into Abergavenny.

Surprisingly King Henry did not punish or remonstrate with William de Braose for his evil act of treachery against the Welsh and he allowed him to retain all his ill-gotten gains. It was not until the young sons of the massacred Welshmen reached fighting age that an act of reprisal was undertaken. In 1182, led by Iorwerth of Caerleon, they attacked Abergavenny Castle and killed or took prisoner the entire garrison. They partially destroyed the castle but no doubt to their disappointment De Braose and his wife, Maud, were not in residence at the time.

After attacking Abergavenny Castle the Welshmen then rode on to Llanddingat (Dingestow), where Ranulph le Poer, Sheriff of Herefordshire, was erecting a castle. They reduced the building to ashes, at the same time killing the Sheriff and nine of his men.

Giraldus Cambrensis, who visited Abergavenny during his travels with Archbishop Baldwin in 1188, stated in his 'Itinerary' that here was *a castle dishonoured by treachery more often than any other in Wales.'* It was just eleven years after the massacre in the Great Hall and Geoffrey in mentioning the incident remarked that *'William de Braose proposed this ordinance to be received of them with corporall oath. That no traveller by the waie amongst them should bear any bow or other lawful weapon, which oath they refused to take, because they would not stand to that ordinance, he condemned them all to death.'*

Giraldus also gives a fascinating description of the wounding of one of De Braose's horsemen during the Welsh attack on the castle. The rider was wounded by an arrow which passed through his armour, his thigh and his saddle, mortally wounding the horse. As the poor animal spun around the man received another arrow through his other thigh and in agony he was fixed firmly to his horse. Such was the power of the Welsh long bow, which is said to have originated in Gwent.

Giraldus also noted that the oak door frame in the castle was *'four fingers thick'* and had been pierced by several arrows. He went on to say that *'the bows used by these people are not made of horn, ivory or yew, but of wild elm, unpolished, rude and uncouth, but stout; not calculated to shoot an arrow to a great distance, but to inflict very severe wounds in a close fight.'*

William de Braose was an ambitious man and he extended his domain in 1191 by giving the king 1000 Marks in return for the wardship of Gilbert of Monmouth. Eleven years later William received permission from King John, who was then on the throne, to possess all the lands that he could conquer from the Welsh. Taking full advantage of this privilege, William added the large estates of the Sitsyllts to his Lordship. Never content, he tried to expand his territory still further and sought possession of Grosmont, Skenfrith and Whitecastle which were collectively known as 'The Trilateral Castles'. He offered King John 800 Marks, three horses, five hunters, 24 hounds and 10 greyhounds in payment, but the king mistrusted the baron's intentions and refused to agree to the deal.

When Maud de Braose, who had a sharp tongue, later insulted King John, he became suspicious of her husband's fidelity and decided to confiscate his estates. William fled to France, leaving Maud to face the king's anger. She refused to hand over her son as hostage, carelessly reminding the king that he had murdered his nephew, Arthur. King John, angered by her brave defiance, came to Abergavenny in 1211 and took Maud and her son, William, as prisoners to Windsor Castle where in a cold dank dungeon they were slowly starved to death.

William de Braose spent the rest of his days in exile, living in a forlorn and penniless state until his death at Corbeuil in Normandy in 1211. His body was taken to Paris and buried in the abbey of St. Victor.

In Abergavenny the de Braose family are represented in stone at St. Mary's Priory Church only by Eva de Braose, the daughter of William Marshall, Earl of Pembroke, and wife of the last William de Braose, Lord of Abergavenny. She died in 1246. The next Lord of Abergavenny was William's son, Giles de Braose, who was also of a violent disposition. He died at Gloucester in 1215 and was buried in the choir of Hereford Cathedral.

After the Great Charter of 1215, King John placed Abergavenny Castle in the hands of a Royal Constable, but the estate was subsequently returned to the de Braose family, who were by that time giving active support to the crown.

This angered Llywelyn ap Iorwerth (Llywelyn Fawr) and he attacked the castle, taking young William de Braose prisoner. This grandson of the infamous Ogre of Abergavenny was taken to Aber Castle in North Wales, where in due course he foolishly had an affair with Llywelyn's wife, Joan, the daughter of King John. When the Welsh prince discovered the intrigue, he reacted by hanging William from a tree within sight of one of the castle windows. Joan suffered a less cruel fate than that of William's grandmother, Maud de Braose, for when she died she was buried at Llanfaes Priory in Anglesey. A coffin lid which is said to bear her image can be seen in the porch of Beaumaris Church.

This William de Braose had four daughters and Maud, the youngest one, married Roger Mortimer, Earl of Wigmore, which meant that two of the most powerful families in the Welsh Marches became related. The Lordship of Abergavenny then passed successively from the De Braose family to those of Cantelupe, Hastings, Beauchamp and finally to the Nevills in the fifteenth century.

If we were able to travel back in time we would find Abergavenny Castle in its finest condition during the 13th and 14th centuries, when it belonged to the Hastings family. One of them became the last Lord of Abergavenny and he was killed whilst jousting at the castle in 1389.

During the Civil War, Abergavenny Castle was held for the king by a garrison commanded by Colonel Proger. In 1645 he received orders from King Charles to make it uninhabitable and thus prevent the enemy forces from making use of it. From that time it became a quarry for stone and over the years many local buildings were constructed from the ruins of the castle.

In the early years of the 20th century garden parties were often held in the castle grounds and on the day of the investiture of Edward VII as Prince of Wales, dinners and teas were provided for no less than 4,288 people. This was a banquet on a massive scale served in three marquees and appropriately in a temporary dining hall erected on the site of the Great Hall where the historic massacre of 1177 took place.

Sugar Loaf and Abergavenny Castle.   *19th Century Engraving*

ROUTE 12

LLANWENARTH CHURCH (4 miles, 2½ hours)

'The extensive parish of Llanwenarth is divided into two portions — viz., Ultra and Citra, by the River Usk, Llanwenarth Ultra includes the village of Govilon with its iron works, and is distant about two and a half miles from Abergavenny. The church is on the Citra side of the river Usk and is dedicated to St. Peter.'

J.H. Clark 1869

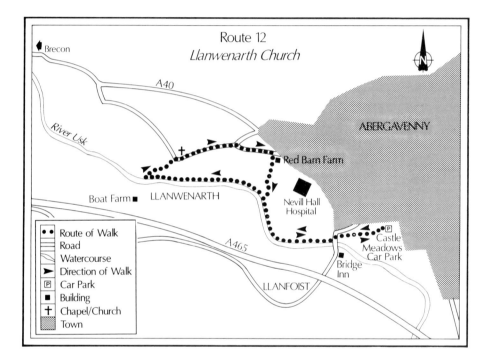

Starting from Abergavenny walk across Castle Meadows to reach Llanfoist Bridge. Cross the road and descend the stone steps beside the bridge and go over a stile. Stop here and look down into the water beside Llanfoist Bridge to see the foundations of the old railway bridge which used to carry the Abergavenny to Merthyr railway. Before that there was a tramroad bridge here. It was built under a special Act of Parliament passed in 1811 and the new tramroad commenced at the Govilon canal wharf, crossed the Usk on a bridge at this spot, continued around to the north of Abergavenny, past the New Inn at Mardy and then ended in a field to the east of Llanfihangel Crucorney. The total length was 7¾ miles. Originally the Llanfihangel Company had intended to build a tramroad all the way to Hereford to transport coal and lime etc. to that town, but obstructions were raised from various vested interests.

74

Old railway bridge over the Usk.   *Albert Lyons Collection*

In 1817 a Special Act was passed for the Grosmont tramroad, which commenced at the terminal of the Llanfihangel tramroad and continued for about 5½ miles to Monmouth Cap at a cost of £12,000. It was not until 1826 that a special Act was passed for the construction of the last length between Monmoth Cap and Hereford of this horse-drawn tramroad and on September 21, 1829 this last stretch was opened and the first consignment of coal was delivered to Hereford from Abergavenny.

In 1843 the Newport, Abergavenny and Hereford Railway Company was formed under a special Act of Parliament to construct a steam railway between Pontypool and Hereford. At this time there were three tramroad companies operating between Abergavenny and Hereford namely, The Llanfihangel Co., The Grosmont., and the Hereford Co., and these were purchased for £21,750, £16,250 and £19,460 respectively. These tramroads appear to have been operated by the Railway Company until the new railway to Hereford was opened on January 2, 1854.

Walk on past the ugly gas pipe arching over the river and continue along a pleasant path to shortly cross a footbridge. Look across to the right and the old Nevill Hall will come into view

Nevill Court and the Sugar Loaf.   *Albert Lyons Collection*

At the beginning of the 18th century a small tenement building called The Brooks belonging to Dr. Samuel Steel stood on this site. In about 1860 it was purchased by Mr. James C. Hill who was one of the proprietors of the Blaenafon Ironworks Company. He demolished the house and spent a large sum of money in building a new one and laying out the gardens. Thirty years later it was purchased by the Marquis of Abergavenny, who re-named it Nevill Court.

In the old days the castle had been the residence of the Lords of Abergavenny but after this fell into decay, the Nevill family did not have an official residence in the town.

The Marquis died in 1915 and the entire estates, with the exception of the castle grounds were sold the following year. Nevill Hall was sold in 1919 to the Board of Management of the Blaina and District Hospital, who bought it for use as a convalescent annexe. However the scheme was abandoned during the industrial depression that followed the 1914-18 War. The property was then leased to a local firm and during the second world war was used by the military. When the National Health Service came into being, the newly appointed North Monmouthshire Management Committee immediately decided that Nevill Hall should be used as a hospital as soon as possible. With the support of the Welsh Regional Board, Nevill Hall became the group medical unit and it opened in January 1953.

A feature of the building is the large number of windows and from these the patients could enjoy excellent views from their beds. When the new hospital was built the old Hall was turned into an administration office.

Cross a stile and continue around a bend of the river. At the time of writing this is a very peaceful spot, but sadly, in the name of 'progress' there are plans for a concrete flyover to be built across the river at this point to carry a new road which will connect the A465 with the A40.

Go over a stile at the end of the field and walk on between a hedge and a fence to reach a footbridge spanning a tributary of the Usk. On the other side, continue with the Sugar Loaf now looming above. Just near here there used to be a monument commemorating a swimmer who drowned in a deep pool at this spot. But it seems to have been washed away by the swirling waters of the Usk.

Llanwenarth Church tower can now be seen directly ahead. Cross another footbridge, go over a stile and walk on through a lovely green field with the escarpment of Mynydd Llangattock dominating the skyline, ahead to the left. Cross another stile and follow the edge of the next field, then go over another stile and follow the fence to the right. The metal post that you can see by the river bank across to the left marks the site of the old ferry crossing.

Go over a stile in a hedge and continue beside a fence to reach another stile. On the other side, turn right along a road to shortly reach Llanwenarth Church.

According to the historian Colonel Bradney the name Llanwenarth *'is compounded of the words Llan Gwen Garth, the church of the blessed enclosure, but the tradition as to the origin of the name is lost. The parish is divided by the River Usk into the hamlets of Llanwenarth Citra and Llanwenarth Ultra and though the church is on the northern side the population has always been on the ultra or southern side.'*

It has also been suggested that the 'wenarth' part of the name comes from Gwen who was the daughter of Arthen a son of Brychan Brycheiniog. She may have founded the first church here at the end of the 6th century but the present building only dates back to 1631 and is dedicated to St. Peter. The churchyard may have once been circular which is an indication that it is certainly an ancient site.

On the square embattled tower is a sundial which is dated 1823 and the top of the tower is capped with a gilded weather cock displaying a plumed tail. There are two bells and one of them is dated 1450.

There is little of interest inside the church apart from its Norman font but in the churchyard are several fascinating gravestones and an ancient base to the churchyard cross which has been restored as a war memorial. Oliver Cromwell's soldiers destroyed the original preaching cross which is believed to be buried nearby.

Walk through the churchyard and continue down the road. Turn right after about ½ mile. Follow this road for about ¼ mile and about 50 yards from Red Barn Farm go over a stile and walk through a field to reach a stile beside a gate. Follow the path through a wood, go over a stile and turn left. Cross another stile and continue beside a stream. Cross another stile and join your outward route by a footbridge. Don't go over the bridge, but follow the riverside path back to Llanfoist Bridge. Cross the road with and return to Abergavenny via Castle Meadows.

ROUTE 13

ASCENT OF THE GRAIG (5 miles, 3 hours)

'Overhanging the Brecon Road is Llanwenarth Breast, one of the south west supporters of the Sugar Loaf. The hill which is dotted with private residences, affords a pleasant climb.'

Wade 1909

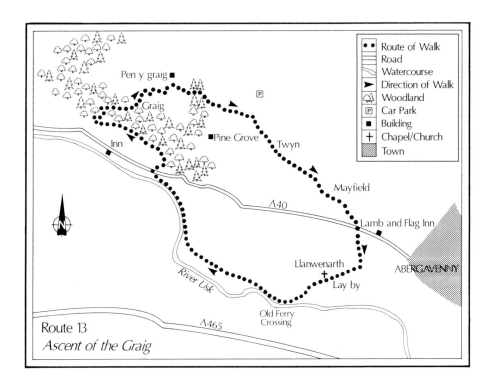

Route 13
Ascent of the Graig

The starting point for this walk is a layby on the left hand side of the road just before Llanwenarth church.

After visiting the church follow the road for a short distance and then go left over a stile by a footpath sign. Continue through a field beside a fence to reach another stile and then go across the next field to reach the river bank. Turn right and after a while you will pass a metal post about 8 feet high with a wheel on the top. On the other side of the river is a white cottage. This is the site of the old ferry crossing.

The River Usk divides the parish of Llanwenarth into two parts and Govilon folk used to cross the river every Sunday to go to church. At one time there was

The old windlas-operated ferry at Llanwenarth.   *Albert Lyons Collection*

a wooden bridge here and the will of Dassie Morgan dated 7th October 1620 instructed that 10s should be left for its repair. But unfortunately the bridge was swept away in a flood so a ferry was introduced instead. It was often a dangerous journey and it is recorded that on one occasion the rope gave way and the fully laden boat was swept down river as far as Llanfoist Bridge. At one time £3 per annum used to be granted from church funds to pay the ferry charges to bring the parishoners across the river. The ferry was operated manually using a cable and pulley and the house on the other side of the river is known as Ferry Cottage.

Continue along the bank to reach another stile. Then cross another field and the path is now some distance from the river bank. Look out for a stile in the hedge on the left. Go over it and turn right to follow a path with the hedge now on your right. Cross a stile close to the river and continue along the river bank.

Go over another stile and bear slightly right, cutting off a bend in the river and passing on your right the buildings of Mardy Farm. Continue past clumps of gorse and on beside a fine stretch of river scenery. To the right now is the densely wooded slope of Graig-rhiw-goch 'the rock of the red ascent.' This name has been abbreviated to Graig. A local inn used to be called Pant-rhiw-goch but this name has been changed to the Llanwenarth Arms.

On seeing an attractive cottage directly ahead, go right up a tarmac ramp to a gate with a stile beside it. Cross the A40 with care and on the other side turn sharp right up a tarmac road which soon leads up through the trees. Just past some cottages go left at a bend and climb a stile beside a gate. Follow the track on the other side and soon you are looking down on a secluded pond. In due course you will observe the remains of cottages half concealed in the trees.

A century ago there were twenty-five freehold cottages constructed on this hillside. The land was given to the poor of the parish by a wealthy benefactress and here they built some humble dwellings. The inhabitants kept donkeys and goats and the Graig became renowned for the production of goats' milk. In addition they grew grapes and figs here which were taken in baskets on the backs of the donkeys to Abergavenny market.

The track traverses the hillside and continues beside a line of electricity pylons. Look out for a short flight of three steps in the bank on the right (Just beyond here, to the left is a stile). Go right up the steps and follow a path diagonally up through the trees. The path crosses a stony area and then meanders through the trees to the right. It leads up to to join a broad track. Turn left here and follow it for about 30 yards and then take a diagonal path leading steeply up to the right.

View of Usk Valley from the lower slopes of Sugar Loaf.   *Chris Barber*

Below now the wooded slope seems very steep and occasionally through the trees you will catch glimpses of the River Usk wending its way towards Abergavenny. The climb seems endless for such an insignificant hill. On reaching a corner look down through the trees to see the Usk heading towards the Blorenge.

From here go straight up to reach a broad track. Cross it and ascend a low bank on the other side. Now continue beside the remains of a stone wall to reach a stile in a fence. On the other side of the stile head straight up across a field, experiencing a sense of relief to be out of the Graig Wood. The hills now start to come back into view; Skirrid Fach, Blorenge and then Sugar Loaf summit pops into sight.

Head towards the right-hand end of the Sugar Loaf to reach a gate. Then continue through the next field and turn left along a track between fences. Go through a gate and turn right at a cross roads, just before a farm. Follow the lane down and at the top of a dingle take a track to the left which leads through the trees and then heads down the left hand side of the dingle. Go through a small gate and follow a stony path. On reaching a junction, keep on the higher path to shortly pass a ruined barn on the right. At a crossing of tracks keep straight on to follow a broad path winding around a little cwm and rising gently above the ruins of an old farmhouse.

Go through a gate and then down beside a fence. You are now looking across to Pine Grove Farm and over the Usk Valley to the Blorenge and Gilwern Hill. Soon you reach a house on the left bearing the motif of the Marquis of Abergavenny (Green Tump Cottage). Now join a tarmac lane and pass below another cottage called The Yew Tree where the occupants enjoy a very impressive view.

At a cross roads, follow the road down to the right to reach a gate. Then on past Twyn Cottage and Twyn Bungalow. Go through another gate and follow a green track leading down beside a fence. The valley floor now seems to come nearer and nearer and below you will see Llanwenarth Church.

Continue through a field, keeping a hedge on the right and continue along a rutted track, past a stately line of trees. Go through a gate and then on down to another gate. Now follow a stony path past some farm buildings. Go left through a gate and continue along a farm drive to shortly pass a group of houses that also bear the emblem of the Marquis of Abergavenny.

At the bottom of the drive go through a gate and carefully cross the A40. Turn right along the pavement and at the end of a stone wall go left and down a bank (watch the ditch at the bottom!). Cross a short field, go over a stile and head left to another stile. Then walk straight across the next field to reach a stile in a hedge. Turn right along the road and make your way back to Llanwenarth Church.

ROUTE 14

ODD CORNERS OF ABERGAVENNY (3 miles, 2 hours)

'Abergavenny occupies a gentle slope, from the foot of the Derry to the left bank of the Usk. The town is long and straggling, and the streets are in general narrow, although within a few years it has been much improved in appearance.'
Archdeacon William Coxe 1801

This is a town walk that has been included to provide a rather circuitous route looking at some of the interesting buildings and features of Abergavenny. It does not include the Castle and St. Mary's Priory Church because they have been described already.

Cross Street, Abergavenny.   *Albert Lyons Collection*

The starting point for the walk is the Town Hall in the centre of Abergavenny. On this site used to stand a Market House, which apparently used to project into the street and cause much inconvenience to the horse and cart traffic. It was built from money left by Philip Jones of Hendre Obaith (where Llanarth Court now stands). In his will dated 1602 he left 200 marks *'to build a market house in Abergavenny after the fashion of the market house in Monmouth, also erected by Philip Jones.'* In the 18th century Jones's Market House was replaced by a new Market Hall and Wool Room designed by the famous architect John Nash. It would seem that he was in the area at the time working on improvements to Kentchurch Court, near Grosmont. For his design of the new Market Hall, Nash received the princely sum of £52 10s and it was built in 1794 by John Knight at a cost of £810. About eighty years later it was pulled down, when the present Town Hall was built.

The tower was built in 1871 by Wilson and Wilcox and its green pyramidal roof is a well known landmark. Crawshay Bailey, the ironmaster donated the clock and it bears a plaque recording the fact that he gave it to the town in 1872. It was manufactured by Messrs Gillett and Bland of Croydon, once a well-known firm of clockmakers. To keep the clock ticking over it takes 500 turns on a large crank handle.

In 1890 a well known local athlete tried to run from the Town Hall to the Swan Hotel before the clock could finish striking twelve. He apparently failed by one strike. This story sounds like a scene out of the film 'Chariots of Fire'. The athlete who took up this challenge was Fred Cooper. He was born in Monk Street, and the town proudly boasted that this man of Abergavenny was the first runner in the world to clock 10 seconds for the 100 yard sprint. In 1898 Fred became the 100 yards amateur champion of Great Britain (10 seconds) and the 100 yards champion of Wales in 1899 (10 seconds). He also played football for the Steam Press, Abergavenny and for Newport Rugby Club. In due course he had a rugby trial to play for England but afterwards signed professional for Bradford Northern Rugby League side. So Fred Cooper was no mean athlete and if he couldn't beat the Town Hall clock then the run to the Swan must surely be impossible in such a time.

Nearly seventy years later Fred Cooper's race against the clock was revived in the form of a novelty event organised by the Abergavenny Holiday Week Committee. It was decided that a race to beat the Town Hall Clock would be held at midnight on 27th June 1959. The distance to the Swan Hotel was measured by M. W.J. Hurst, the Borough Engineer and found to be 810 feet or 270 yards. An accurate measurement of the time that it took the clock to strike twelve was also made and found to be exactly 27.5 seconds.

Abergavenny folk waited with considerable excitement for the day of the race to arrive. It was held on a Saturday night and by 20 minutes to midnight there were some two thousand people lining Cross Street on both sides of the road to watch a dozen athletes participate in this unusual event. The spectators heard the clock strike a quarter to twelve and the excitement grew but the twelve o'clock strike failed to happen. The hand ceased to move at 11.47 precisely and cries of 'The clock has stopped!' rang through the night air, whilst other saw the funny side of the situation and laughed until they cried.

The race against Crawshay Bailey's clock had to be abandoned of course, but the perplexed organisers persuaded the bewildered competitors to race down to the Swan so that there could at least be a winner for the crowd to cheer to victory.

Everyone was of course asking the same questions. 'Did old faithful stop of its own accord? or had there been some dirty work afoot?' The last time that the clock had stopped was in 1912, when it was struck by lightning.

On the Monday morning, Mr. Wells, manager of Messrs Rowe and Sons, the firm responsible for the maintenance of the clock, climbed the Town Hall stairs and went into the back of the balcony to investigate. He discovered that some joker had tied the pendulum with a black shoe lace to the door of the cupboard.

Later on it was pointed out that the two thousand strong crowd were making so much noise that no one would have heard the clock striking anyway. If the race was ever run again, the sound would have to be amplified!

Another memorable day at the Town Hall was Friday, May 10th, 1963, when The Queen and the Duke of Edinburgh paid the town a visit. This was surprisingly the first time that a reigning monarch had come to the town since Charles I in 1645.

They arrived in driving rain at Abergavenny Road Station, where they were welcomed by Lord Raglan, the Lord Lieutenant of Monmouthshire. From there they were driven up gaily decorated Cross Street to the Town Hall, where they were received by the Mayor. As they climbed the flower-lined steps to enter the freshly decorated Council Chamber the Mayor apologised to the Queen for the lack of a traditional red carpet. When she was told of the Council decision to paint the steps with red liquid linoleum she remarked with a smile, 'I think it's a wonderful idea.'

An Abergavenny man who was temporarily living in Malaya wrote to the local paper a few weeks later to say that he was disgusted to read that Abergavenny Town Council were unable to afford to buy a red carpet for the Queen's visit. He thought that after the large amount of money recently spent on a new recreation ground, surely the Town Council could have *scraped together sufficient money to obtain some sort of a carpet.*' As a loyal townsman he enclosed £1 to start a public collection to help the *'overt stricken'* Town Council to be prepared for the next Royal visit.

Just over a month later the Town Hall had some more famous visitors. The Beatles, Britain's number one pop group had been booked to appear on the 22nd of June, and the town was full of fans clamouring for a glimpse of the 'fab four.'

John Lennon the lead guitarist was flown to the venue from the BBC television studios in London after making a tele-recorded appearance on Juke Box Jury. His helicopter landed in Bailey Park.

Paul McCartney had celebrated his 21st birthday a few days before the dance and on the Saturday night at the Town Hall he was presented with a huge birthday card signed by hundreds of those present. In fact, there were over 500 supporters who had travelled from widespread places such as Cheltenham, Newport, Ebbw Vale, Chepstow, Cwmbran and Pontypool, on special coaches which had been specially laid on for the occasion. Yes, Abergavenny well remembers that night when the Beatles were in town!

Having given consideration to some of the Town Hall history, it is now time to start the walk.

Go up Market street, which is the narrow street with the raised footway going past the side of the Town Hall. After you have gone a short way, look back to observe the north face of the Town Hall clock which is painted black on this one side to commemorate the death of Prince Albert, who passed away in 1861.

At one time this street was known as Traitor's Lane and this name is said to stem from the occasion way back in 1404, when Owain Glyndwr besieged the town. A woman who sympathised with his cause opened the town gate near this spot and admitted the Welsh forces, who immediately went on the rampage, sacking and burning the timber buildings. It was certainly a dark time for Abergavenny during which the town was practically destroyed and it lost all its mili-

Market Street, once known as Traitor's Lane.   *Chris Barber*

tary importance. For nearly a century it lay derelict, but then gradually the buildings were reconstructed and the town had a peaceful existence until Oliver Cromwell paid a visit to crush a revolt of Royalist sympathisers. His soldiers damaged many buildings and even vandalised the old Priory Church, using the antique woodwork of the stalls to construct enclosures for their horses. Shortly afterwards the town lost its Charter which was not renewed until 1899.

You will shortly pass the Greyhound Vaults on the left and then the strangely-named 'Ant and Rubber Plant Restaurant.' Further ahead are the more traditional 'Farmers' Arms' and 'The Black Lion.' Directly ahead can be seen Abergavenny Cattle Market which is one of the largest in South Wales. This was erected in 1863 on the site of the old town cricket pitch. At one time Abergavenny used to have six annual fairs and two weekly markets. The latter still take place, and on Tuesdays and Fridays the town is bursting with life.

Turn left past the Black Lion and then shortly cross the road and go down a lane between a shop and the boundary wall of the Cattle Market. It brings you out opposite the Fairfield Car Park. Cross the road and turn right along the pavement.

Looking through the gateway of Bailey Park.   *Albert Lyons*

Shortly go left to pass through some iron gates and enter Bailey Park. Follow a tarmac lane through an avenue of trees at the south end of the park, enjoying the view up through the Park towards the Sugar Loaf and the rounded hump of Deri. In the distance can also be seen the summit of Skirrid Fawr.

Before this was established as a park it was known as the Priory Meadow and in 1871 the Abergavenny Bicycle Club secured an area of land here for use as a cycle racing track. It was a ¼ mile long and cyclists wishing to make use of the circuit had to pay a few pence which went towards the rental charge for the land.

It was several years later that Bailey Park was opened. This is of course named after Crawshay Bailey the son of the famous Ironmaster and the park was laid out at his expense after he had taken a long lease on the site. When it was opened on August 6th 1883, Crawshay Bailey Junior was in Brighton and he died a few years later at the age of 46. The town purchased the freehold of the park in 1894 from the Rev. W.W. Roberts for £5,000 and of this amount £3,250 was paid out of the rates. The other half was contributed by the trustees of the Bailey estate.

Annual Abergavenny Steam Rally.   *Abergavenny Chronicle*

Every Whitsun the annual Abergavenny Steam Rally is held in Bailey Park and it ranks as the eighth largest Steam Rally in Britain, attracting participants from some considerable distance away.

Leave the park by the main gates, cross the Hereford Road and turn right along the pavement. Take the next road on the left which is called Lower Monk Street. This name is derived from the fact that St. Mary's Priory and its manor used to be known as Monktown or Monkswick.

In Lower Monk Street there used to be a pub called the Omar Pasha. It was kept by a Mr. Roberts who was a well-known local character and became the headquarters of a branch of the Ancient Order of Foresters of which he was a prominent member. A popular event during the year was the annual parade of the Foresters in picturesque uniforms representing Robin Hood and his merry men. Roberts took the part of Robin Hood, but he was blind in one eye and wore a black patch, so local people always laughed and said the he looked more like a bucaneer than the famous hero of Sherwood Forest.

The road drops down into a dip where you go right and enter a pleasant little park.

Go left over a rustic bridge and follow the bank of the rippling Cybi Brook. This is of course named after the sixth-century St. Cybi who came to Wales from Cornwall. Looking to the right you will catch glimpses of the noble tower of St. Mary's Church.

At the end of the park a path leads up beside a hand rail to reach a metal gate. Turn left and go up Holywell Road, following the pavement. After about 100 yards cross the road to look at a stone trough set into a low wall. This part of the town was once known as Holy Well, which was sometimes corrupted to Hole-in-the Wall. Here you will see a stone trough fed by springs. Long ago it was the water supply for the Benedictine Priory and said to have healing powers. In those times it would have of course been situated in a field as part of land owned by the priory. In 1825 the Rev John Thomas who had been an Usher at King Henry VIII Grammar School died suddenly after drinking water from this well but it may have just been a coincidence ! The horse trough that you see here today was constructed by an Abergavenny builder — Mr. Foster and nearby Fosterville Crescent is named after him.

Other ancient wells in Abergavenny included; St.Lawrence's Well near the cemetery on the old Hereford Road, St. Mary's Well near the Priory Mill, Priory Well in Bailey Prody, Pant's Well below Pant Lane and a well or spout in Byfield Lane.

Go back down to the main road and taking special care, go straight across, to pass the Abergavenny Hotel. Continue up Mill Street, and head towards the 'keep' of Abergavenny Castle. You will pass on the left a small industrial estate and it is interesting to think that this street was once the main thoroughfare into the town and it of course takes its name from the Mill that used to stand here. Records show that there was a grist mill here in 1679 and the last waterwheel in Mill Street was demolished in the 1960's. The existing waterwheel that you will notice on the left was erected as a feature by Mr. Ray Jones in memory of the tradespeople who worked in Mill Street in days gone by and a plaque informs you that on this site once stood Rees's Corn Mill.

At one time there was a considerable range of different industries in Abergavenny and its neighbourhood. Hides were cured and processed in local tanneries and wool from the sturdy mountain sheep was spun and woven into cloth in local factories and cottages. Local timber was used for making pit props and for the production of charcoal. There was once a boot factory in the town, a hat works, two candle factories, two iron foundries, a wire works and a paper mill.

Turn right and shortly cross the road to follow the pavement towards the Swan Hotel and then turn left up Cross Street.

An interesting building on the other side of the road is Trekitt's the outdoor equipment shop. This is part of a building that used to be known as the Gunter Mansion which in the seventeenth century it was occupied by Thomas Gunter.

He was an attorney and a leading Roman Catholic who during the days of the Titus Oates Plot, allowed public services to be held in a secret chapel in his house. Two priests, Father David Lewis (son of a teacher at King Henry VIII Grammar School) and Father Phillip Evans officiated in this chapel but both were subsequently hanged, drawn, quartered and burnt in 1679.

On the wall of the Coach and Horses you will notice a plaque marking the 'Site of Medieval Town Gate.' This was the East Gate to the town.

At the corner of Monk Street is the Great George Inn, which has an unusual sign, depicting George Washington the first president of the American republic on one side and George Bernard Shaw the great Irish dramatist, who made such a mark with his wit, on the other. It is unusual to have a different picture on each side of a pub sign.

Beneath the Great George in the cellars is an entrance to an ancient underground passage. This hotel lies within the former medieval town wall, close to the East Gate.

Angel Hotel, Cross Street.   *Chris Barber*

On your left you will pass the Angel Hotel, a fine Georgian building, which is the largest hotel in Abergavenny where many important functions and meetings are held. This was once an important coaching inn on the road to Milford Haven. In 1858 this route came to an end, but the Angel became the terminus of a daily service from Ross in the 1890's.

An 1835 Timetable provided the following information:—

To London, the Royal Mail (from Milford) calls at the Angel, every forenoon at 20 mins, past eleven. The 'Nimrod' (from Brecon) every morning (Sunday accepted) at half past nine.

To Brecon, the 'Nimrod' (from London) calls at the Angel, every afternoon (Sunday excepted) at quarter past one.

To Hereford, a coach from the Angel every afternoon at four.

To Milford, the 'Royal Mail' (from London) calls at the Angel every afternoon at two; goes through Crickhowell, Brecon etc.

To Newport, the 'Royal Mail' (from London) calls at the Angel every morning at eight; goes through Pontypool and Caerleon.

There is a courtyard at the rear of the building into which the Royal Mail Coach drove through an archway in the Cross Street side of the hotel.

A fancy dress ball held here in the 'Great Room' in 1838 was attended by two hundred ladies and gentlemen from most of the influential families of the neighbourhood, including Sir Benjamin Hall and his wife Lady Llanover and Crawshay Bailey the ironmaster.

The Morgan family once resided at the Angel Hotel and one of their sons was Walter Morgan who is worthy of a mention for he is the only Abergavenny man who has ever become Mayor of London, and could thus be described as the local Dick Whittington ! In 1846 when he was just 15 years old he left Abergavenny and went to work in London at the office of the National Provincial Cashier of England. He was appointed Sheriff in 1900, Lord Mayor of London in 1905 and was subsequently knighted.

Many famous people have stayed or dined at the Angel Hotel over the years. One noted film star who has been here is Gregory Peck who stopped for a meal in August 1954 He was accompanied by the well-known director, John Houston when they were en route to Fishguard in West Wales, to spend eight weeks filming 'Moby Dick.' Peck was then 38 years old and wore a heavy beard specially grown for the sea-faring role as Captain Ahab. This was his first visit to Wales.

You may also be interested to know that Queen Victoria once passed through Abergavenny on her way to Haverfordwest. She was only a slip of a girl at the time and she stood for a while outside the Angel Hotel, while the horses were changed on her coach.

At one time youngsters in Abergavenny used to think up riddles about Cross Street. They used to ask with a smile, 'Why is Cross Street like the River Usk ?'

Answer: 'Because there is a bank on either side !'

Or, 'Why is Cross Street like the heavens?'

Answer: 'Because there's a Sun, a Moon and an Angel in it'. (Names of one-time pubs and the existing Angel Hotel).

In the first half of the nineteenth century Abergavenny had over fifty inns for during that period it became a particularly busy and thriving town. Pub names such as The Dog and Bull, the Blue Feathers, The Wellington, the Crown and the Parrot, which all used to stand in Cross Street are now nothing but a very distant memory. On the site of the Town Hall used to stand two inns which were demolished to make way for it. They were the Plume of Feathers and the Dog and Bull. Other vanished pubs include the London Apprentice Inn, the Mason's Arms, the Haulier's Arms, the Duke of Cumberland, the Earl Grey, the Blackamoor's Head, the Raven Hotel, the Unicorn and the Green Dragon. Following the arrival in 1854, of the first steam train from Pontypool to Hereford several new inns were opened near the Monmouth and Brecon Road Stations. But for many more years the horse remained the principal means of transport and the larger inns kept post horses, hunters and carriages and even sent their own omnibuses to meet the trains.

Cross Street, Abergavenny.   *Albert Lyons Collection*

It is interesting that all the streets in Abergavenny used to be very narrow, with the exception of Cross Street which was used by the Castle garrison for drilling purposes. There used to be a stone cross at the top of Cross Street, near the present Town Hall. The base of the cross is probably the large block of stone that can be seen in the garden of rest adjoining St. Mary's Priory Church.

In 1881 Abergavenny was struck by a severe snow storm and in the Abergavenny Chronicle it was recorded that, *'about 11 o'clock one Wednesday morning a strange-looking craft was observed struggling in clouds of snow that drifted with intense violence up Cross Street and in the lull of the gale it was discovered to be Mr. Crawshay Bailey's sleigh drawn by two horses and containing Mr. and Mrs. Bailey and two attendants. After several stoppages before the mountains of snow which obstructed their passage, Mr. Bailey managed to pilot his team along High Street down Lion Street and into the safe shelter afforded in the Greyhound yard.'*

On the right you will see the King's Head Hotel with its medieval Gothic archway, giving access to a cobbled courtyard, where there used to be a medieval corn market. A one-time landlord of the King's Head was James Cole whose claim to fame was the fact that he sat on the jury at the trial of John Frost the Chartist leader at Monmouth in 1839.

You have now arrived back at the Town Hall so if you have had enough of tramping the streets of Abergavenny, you may decide to finish the walk here. But if you wish to complete the second half of this mystery tour then take the next turning on the left, which is called Flannel Street.

Hen and Chickens, Flannel Street.   *Chris Barber*

It is known by this name because Welsh flannel used to be produced here, for which the town was famous. The surrounding hills were ideal for sheep breeding to produce a fine species of wool. However the industry declined and moved to Newtown in Montgomeryshire where they still produced 'Abergavenny flannel' in 1800.

Following the loss of its flannel industry Abergavenny looked for commercial salvation in the manufacture of periwigs, which for a while were the height of fashion. However this trade did not prove very profitable for once a gentleman bought a wig he didn't seem to mind how dirty it became and went on wearing it for several years. The Abergavenny periwigs were sometimes sold for as much as 40 guineas each but within a short time, change of fashion caused this business to be abandoned in the middle of the eighteenth century. A petition was even sent to George III in 1765 emphasising the distress that the wig-makers were now in, for the nobility and people of high class were now wearing their own hair instead of wigs made from the hair of Welsh goats. This was followed by a humorous petition to the king from the 'Body of Carpenters' who implored him to have one of his legs amputated so that he might popularise the fashion of wearing a wooden leg and encourage the manufacture of such items!

However, before too long the Industrial Revolution arrived and mines and ironworks were rapidly established just over the other side of the Blorenge bringing prosperity back to the town.

Flannel Street was also known at one time as Butcher's Row because of the number of butchers' shops located there. The cellar of the present butcher's shop is lined with gravestones from the old St. John's Church graveyard, which covered quite a large area.

An interesting old pub in Flannel Street is the 'Hen and Chickens'. It was here that the Newport born tramp poet W. H. Davies once spent an inebriated night in 1911 and wrote:—

'O what a merry world I see
Before me through a quart of ale.'

At one time Flannel Street was twice as long as it is today. Sadly many houses here and in other streets were condemned and pulled down during the Borough Council's slum clearance scheme during the late 1950's and early 1960's.

To your right you will see the tower of St. John's Church. This was the first parish church in Abergavenny, until the Dissolution of the Monasteries when St. Mary's Priory became the Parish Church. In 1536, Henry VIII's Grammar School was founded utilising the revenues from the Priory in the old parish church of St. Johns. The king directed that a competent master should be appointed to the school at a yearly salary of £13 6s 8d and that he should be assisted by an Usher who would receive a yearly salary of £6 13s 4d. According to Henry's charter, the master was required to accept any boy into the school who possessed an acceptable level of intelligence. The school flourished here for over 350 years and in 1898 it was moved to new buildings in Pen-y-Pound which were erected at a cost of more than £6,000

At one time a curfew bell was hung in St. John's Church and it was rung to announce the closing of the town gates. It used to be claimed that there was a passage from St. John's Church which was inside the town wall to St. Mary's

Church outside it. Dr. Steel of Abergavenny is said to have claimed that when he was a boy his father found a secret passage from St. John's Church to the castle, at the bottom of his garden.

Turn right and follow the stone wall around to the left along St. John's Lane which was once known as Chicken Street. The old tower of St. John's Church is now incongruously welded to a villa like building which is used as a Masonic Temple. In St. John's Lane is a very fine Tudor doorway and here can be seen one of the many plaques erected by the Abergavenny Local History Society to indicate buildings of special interest in the town.

Continue beside the wall following a pedestrianised lane which brings you to Neville Street which has also been pedestrianised. Turn left and walk past the British Legion which was once the Dragon's Head Inn. During alterations, some years ago a crude painting of an heraldic lion was exposed on one of the plastered walls.

Neville Street was originally called Rother Street and No.11 is still known as Rother House. The word Rother means 'horned cattle' but the breed of Rother cattle is now extinct. At one time a cattle market used to be held in this street. The cattle were driven from West Wales and put to graze on Castle Meadows for a few days. They were then driven up Byfield Lane,to Rother Street. From here they were driven to the markets in the Midlands and England.

Old Cow Inn, Nevill Street.   *Chris Barber*

Further on, stop outside the very attractive shop of Charles Price. This used to be the old Cow Inn which had one entrance in Nevill Street and another in St. John's Square. The arms of the Vaughan Family of Tretower Court can be seen

94

on the window mouldings and consisting of a chevron with three childs' heads with necks encircled by serpents. The Vaughan family were descendants of Ynyr, King of Gwent in the 6th century. Sir Roger Vaughan was knighted by King Henry V on the battlefield at Agincourt and Henry Vaughan was one of the early headmasters of King Henry VIII Grammar School in 1654.

A plaque on the wall informs the visitor . . . *'16th century house of the Vaughan family, became the Cow Inn in the 18th century.'*

Its name is confirmed by a row of brightly coloured bovine heads under the projecting soffit of the roof. Here the drovers came for refreshment and to strike a bargain with purchasers of their cattle.

Continue to enter St. John's Square.

The Bull Inn used to stand on the site of the present Post Office. Talking of bulls, Abergavenny was once noted for its breed of bull-dogs which were reputed to never loose their hold on a bull's nose until the beast had rolled over on its back. At one time bull baiting was a popular sport in the town and on one occasion a bull that had killed a man, was in accordance with tradition, run through the streets and baited thoroughly to the danger of the spectators near the Bull Inn. The bull-ring was probably near the inn but it is possible that the Bull Inn did not get its sign from an actual bull but from the coat of arms of one of the local nobility.

King's Arms, Nevill Street.   *Chris Barber*

Across the street on the right is the King's Arms which is associated with Charles I. During the Civil War King Charles paid his first visit to Abergavenny on his journey from Hereford on Ist July 1645 after the Royalists' big defeat at the battle of Naseby. He stayed two nights at the Priory and gave orders for the castle to be made untenable. He then went on to Raglan Castle and returned on September 8th to see the results and *'to try five hinderers, who were slow in going to the relief of Hereford.'*

By the end of 1645, Abergavenny was held by the Roundheads and on January 24th, the town was attacked by a Royalist force from Raglan led by Lord Charles Somerset, but the attack failed and fifty Royalists were taken prisoner by the Roundheads.

On the front of the King's Arms can be seen a plaster plaque displaying the coat of Arms of Charles I, in memory of an occasion when he stayed there. But this pub was probably built some two centuries before then.

Charles I was the last monarch to visit Abergavenny Castle and before him royal visitors included King John who made a brief visit in 1211, King Henry III in 1233 and Edward I who held a council there which lasted three weeks in 1291.

George IV once passed through Abergavenny on his way from Haverfordwest to Monmouth. The townsfolk who watched him pass through were bitterly disappointed that he did not stop and some of his escort of yeomanry were apparently exhausted by his rapid pace, almost to the point of collapse.

There used to be a stone at Abergavenny Cottage hospital commemorating the visit on 17th March 1932 of the Duke and Duchess of York who later became King George V and Queen Mary. The visit of Queen Elizabeth II and Prince Phillip in May 1963, has already been mentioned.

Turning our thoughts back to the King's Arms it is interesting that it once served as Abergavenny's first post office, and it was also a noted house of call for stage coaches. On one of the oak beams inside the pub are carved the names of soldiers of the King's Own (15th) Hussars who were quartered here in 1817, two years after the battle of Waterloo. In 1862 the pub was taken over by a Thomas Delafield and according to one old advertisement 'it soon enjoyed a high reputation for Delafield's pure ales and stouts obtainable in any quantities from a half-pint bottle to a 54 gallon cask.'

Turn right past the King's Arms and observe on the other side of the road the 'Old Court' where a plaque on the wall bears the words 'Medieval West Gate'.

When Archdeacon Coxe came here in 1801 the four town gates were still standing and also the greater part of the old town wall.

After a few more yards look down a narrow alleyway to your right to see an ivy-covered remnant of the old town wall. The West Gate or Tudor Gate was described by Archdeacon Coxe as 'a strong gothic portal, defended by a portcullis of which the groove is visible.' It was named Tudor Gate after Jasper Tudor the uncle of Henry VII who was made Constable of Abergavenny.

This was the last survivor of the town's four gates and it was pulled down in the early 19th century by the Abergavenny Improvement Commisioners.

From here the wall continues very much in its original state at the back of the houses on the west side of Nevill Street and the North Gate was where the Midland Bank in Frogmore Street stands. The wall then carried on round to the right and a section can be seen where it meets Market Street and now forms the wall of a cottage garden. Here stood the East Gate or Monks' Gate. In this gateway used to be a lock up for prisoners and beneath the building flowed the Cybi

Brook. A sensation was caused in the 19th century by a prisoner who one night raised the paving-stones and gained his liberty by crawling out along the bed of the brook.

This lock up had a massive oak door studded with large nails and a substantial lock and keyhole. About 130 years ago a local character well known for his passion for drink was regularly locked up there. His sympathetic friends used to render 'first aid' in an amusing way. They obtained a jug of beer from a neighbouring pub, put the stem of a big church warden pipe through the keyhole and poured the beer down the pipe. With such good friends to make him feel at home, a night in the clink certainly had its attractions for this fellow.

Go past the Tudor Gate Surgery and cross the road. Then opposite the Magistrate's Court go left down a road leading to a car park. Head around to the right and go through a metal gate hung on pillars which bear the words 'Linda Vista 1865'

Turn left and follow a path through the gardens. 'Linda Vista' is Spanish for 'beautiful view' and these gardens were once the grounds of Lind Vista — built in 1870's. It was Mrs. Whitehead who established the gardens assisted by her gardening staff. Some of the more interesting trees include a flowering cherry tree, a copper beech tree, a tulip tree and a Californian Red Wood.

The gardens were taken over by Abergavenny Borough Council in 1974 and they are now owned and maintained by Monmouth Borough Council.

Make your way up to another set of gates and come out on the pavement in Tudor Street. With the exception of the Old Court and Linda Vista all the historic buildings in Tudor Street were pulled down in the late 1950's as part of the town's now much regretted slum clearance scheme. A building of special interest was the Elizabethan Bell Inn which contained curved tree roof timbers, partitions of wattle and daub and several late Tudor fireplaces, one of which was re-erected in the museum.

The Cymreigyddion Hall used to stand in Tudor Street and it was used by the Cymdeithas Cymreigyddion y Fenni (The Society of Welsh Scholars of Abergavenny). This society was established in Abergavenny during 1883 for the purpose of encouraging Welsh literature, harp playing and the native industries of making woollens and hats. On the 22nd of November, in 1833 twenty-five Welshmen of the town and neighbourhood met at the Sun Inn to officially found the society. Within three months seventy-five members had been enrolled and the society was honoured with the patronage of Sir Charles Morgan of Tredegar, Mr. Hall of Llanover (who afterwards became Sir Benjamin Hall, and finally Lord Llanover), and by the gentry of the county generally. Impressive prizes, ranging from £100 to £1, were awarded for subjects in prose and verse, for playing the harp and also for making woollen hats. The society obtained the Cymreigyddion Hall in about 1840. It was of substantial capacity, capable of seating 2,000 people and meetings held here were attended by distinguished persons from all parts of Wales and even Brittany.

On October 11 and 12 in 1848, an Eisteddfod was held here under the patronage of the Prince of Wales. Colonel Kemeys Tyme was president of the meeting and among the people present were Lady Hall of Llanover, the Marquis of Northampton, Angharad Llwyd, Chevalier Bunsen of Prussia, Calimaki of Turkey and Lady Charles Somerset. A prize of 25 guineas was given by the Prince of Wales for the best critical essay on the language and literature of Wales from the time of Gruffyd ab Cynon and Meilyr to that of Gruffyd Llwyd and Gwilym Ddu. It was won by Thomas Stephens of Merthyr and the essay was subsequently published under the title 'The Literature of the Cymry.'

As the town became more English in speech and sentiment, these meetings came to an end in about 1853. However twenty years later a large Eisteddfod was held in the town at the new Market House under the patronage of Crawshay Bailey.

Many visitors to the town are intrigued by the site of what they take to believe a large 'prehistoric stone circle' situated behind a wall, on the left hand side of the Monmouth road, going out of Abergavenny. It is in fact a Bardic Circle erected for the Welsh National Eistedfodd, which was held in Abergavenny in 1913. A prize was offered on this occasion for the best-made Welsh harp and it was won by two men from Llanover. It would seem that Llanover was the last place in Wales where harps were made. Since the 10th century this instrument had special status for Welsh law decreed that it was the only household possession that could not be seized for debt.

Follow Tudor Street up to the Merthyr Road. Cross with considerable care and make your way up Union Road East. At the end of the road go over a metal footbridge to cross above the industrial link road built along the route of the old railway to Merthyr.

The L.N.W.R. Loco Sheds, 1952.   *Albert Lyons*

Abergavenny is not only famous as a market town but it was once was once the railway centre of South Wales. During World War I railway activity in Abergavenny reached its peak with over 1,000 men employed at Brecon Road and Abergavenny Junction. Some 450 of them were engine-men of all grades who worked the 100 or so engines in the sheds. In 1941 some 40 firemen were made redundant in one day and this started the general decline. Then came nationalisation and the S. Wales division lost its independence to become part of the Western Region.

In those times Abergavenny was alive with a symphony of railway sounds remembered by many with nostalgia — the clang of hammers, the hiss of steam, whistles hooting and wheels clattering over joints and points.

Here could be seen magnificent locos in the old LNWR livery of black and red with gold bands. They ranged from the sturdy tankers which worked the Merthyr and the Valleys line to the giants to whom such names as Crewe and Carlisle and Glasgow were everyday words. Day in and day out they came into the engine sheds for service and left gleaming.

When the Merthyr Tredegar & Abergavenny line closed to goods traffic on 22nd November, 1954, out of the 250 men employed at the Abergavenny engine shed, 200 were made redundant.

Shortly on the right you will pass the old Abergavenny Workhouse (The Union). During the period 1838 -1930 this was where you had to go if you had no money or job or someone to take you in.

The first workhouse in Abergavenny was at the other end of town in Mill Street, built as a result of the Poor Law Amendment Act.

The workhouse in Union Road was at one time well outside the town but over the years Abergavenny increased substantially in size and the building became absorbed into the town. It used to have a bell tower and the bell was rung to wake up the residents in the morning and summon them to meals. The bell is now in Abergavenny Museum. Originally Union Road was called Brook's Lane.

Take the next turning on the right and pass around the rear of the Workhouse complex of buildings, now used for a variety of small businesses. Go left down a lane and straight across a road at the bottom to follow the pavement beside the road directly opposite. Notice some houses on the right bearing the distinctive motif of the Marquis of Abergavenny.

On reaching the Brecon Road, turn right along the pavement. Cross the road at a safe moment and follow the pavement on the other side, now heading back towards the centre of Abergavenny. Go past the Cantref Inn which is named after a suburb of Abergavenny called Cantreff. At one time it consisted of just an inn and a few adjoining cottages. Now cross over the bottom of Chapel Road. Continue along the pavement passing The Railway Inn on the right and The Station Inn on the left. These two pubs are also reminders of the railway age in Abergavenny, for near here used to be the Brecon Road Station.

Walk on to reach the Abergavenny Baptist Church which is built in the Romanesque style with a central rose window. However it has sometimes been said to resemble a Victorian engine house!

From here we look across to the War Memorial.

Memorial to the 3rd Mons Battalion.   *Chris Barber*

At a public meeting held in the Town Hall on Tuesday April 28th, 1919 it was recommended that £1,000 be spent on an 'enduring and artistic monument which shall record all the names of them of Abergavenny who have given their lives in the war.'

The result was a regimental memorial in memory of the 3rd Mons and it was erected as a result of subscriptions from the people of Abertillery, Ebbw Vale, Cwm, Tredegar, Rhymney and Abergavenny. This bronze figure of a weary looking infantryman of the Third Battalion in the Monmouthshire Regiment leans on his rifle gazing at the passing traffic and the Tesco-bound shoppers. It is a fine monument, realistic in every detail, even to the mud on his boots. The sculptor was Gilbert Ledward R.G.A. of London and his work was unveiled in the presence of 4-5,000 people.

Abergavenny's official memorial to the dead of World War I took the form of an additional wing at the Victoria Cottage Hospital, built from money collected from local people who also paid for the plaque at the foot of the Town Hall steps.

Follow the road around to the left and shortly pass on the right the Abergavenny Drama Centre which was originally the second King Henry VIII Grammar School building after St. John's Church became too small for the number of pupils.

Soon on the left you will see the Catholic Church of Our Lady and St. Michael, designed by Benjamin Bucknell and built in 1858-60. A very fine Calvary figure stands on the bank near the entrance. Inside the church is an elaborate reredos with a choir of angels. The east window fills the entire wall of the chancel and depicts the figures of St. Thomas, St. Benedict, the Madonna and child, Joseph, St. Scholastica and St. Margaret of Scotland. The church also has a painting of St. Michael slaying a Devil. This is the work of Kenelm Digby, who was killed during the Civil War at the battle of St. Neots in 1648.

Preserved in the church is a rescript of Pope Clement X dated 1676 granting a plenary indulgence to those who visited the chapel of St. Michael on the summit of Skirrid Fawr on the Feast of St. Michael and All Angels on September 29th each year.

Pen-y-Pound Toll House.   *Chris Barber*

Continue to reach the old Pen-y-Pound toll house which was built in 1831 and recently enlarged and restored. In the 1800's an Act was passed by the Government which allowed land-owners to erect these houses on the town boundary and collect a toll. During the Rebecca Riots this toll house was stoned and the rioters charged through the gate into the centre of Abergavenny.

At one time it was impossible to enter or leave Abergavenny without paying a toll for there were similar toll houses and gates situated at the junction of Merthyr Road and Tudor Street, at the junction of Brecon Road and Chapel Road, at the junction of Monmouth Road and Station Road, at the corner of Holywell Road where it meets Lower Monk Street and at the corner of Hereford Road and Croesonnen Road.

Go across Avenue Road, bear right along the pavement. Look up towards the Sugar Loaf and below the left hand side of the Deri can be seen the Hill Residential College. Here a wide selection of weekend courses are available in comfortable and congenial surroundings.

This part of the town is called Pen-y-Pound and the name means the pond head (pound being used in colloquial Welsh for a pond). A small reservoir fed by the Cybi Brook used to be sited in the kitchen garden of a house called the Willows.and for many years water was conveyed from here in pipes to various parts of the town. A poor donkey once fell into the reservoir and came to an untimely end.

Pen-y-Pound House was once occupied by Dr. Samuel Hopkins Steel and the name was later changed to Dyne House after Dyne Steel. This family originally came from the Forest of Dean and were for over half a century the chief medical men in the town. The family graves can be seen in Llanfoist churchyard.

Cross the old Hereford Road and go down a lane leading past a stone wall. On reaching a road junction go straight across and turn right along the pavement. Continue past Abergavenny Labour Club, cross Skirrid Road and head down Pen-y-Fal Road. On reaching the junction with Park Road, go straight across and follow the pavement to the left. Go past the builder's yard and take the next turning on the right. This leads past the rear of the yard and past some public toilets, to reach Frogmore Street. Turn left and follow the pavement.

Look back for a good view of the Baptist church dominating the end of Frogmore Street. When the road bends to the left, go straight across and follow the pedestrianised street back to the Town Hall.

ROUTE 15

UP THE RIVER AND DOWN THE CANAL (3½ miles, 2½ hours)

This walk starts from Llanfoist Bridge. You may be able to park on the side of the road just before the Bridge Inn or alternatively park in the large car park adjoining Castle Meadows and walk across the fields to reach Llanfoist Bridge.

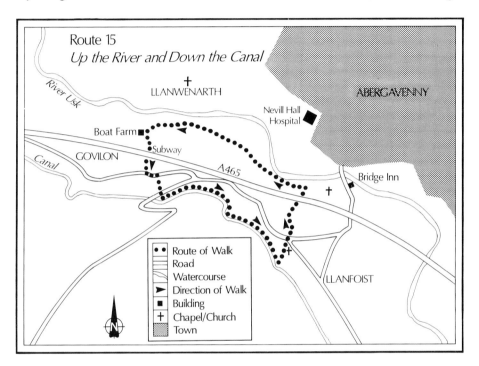

At the Llanfoist end of the bridge, cross the road and go up the lane past the cemetery. On reaching a left hand bend go right over a stile and follow a gravel driveway down to pass a house in a pleasant setting beside the river. (In due course a road scheme may change this beautiful spot, but that is progress, as they say!)

Go over a stile beside a gate and across a field to reach the river bank. Turn left and follow the bank for a short· way, enjoying the view across the rippling water towards the Sugar Loaf. Then go over a stile beside a gate and leave the river bank and bear left to reach another stile. Continue with a fence on your right to reach a stile beneath an oak tree. Walk on with the fence now on your left.

At the end of the fence go over a stile and continue with the fence now on your right to reach a stile near a gate. Head straight across the next field. Negotiate another stile, cross a cart track and immediately go over yet another stile.

Keep straight on with the fence now on your right to cross a rutted track and continue to a stile in the corner of the field. By now the summit of the Sugar Loaf has disappeared, but the two Skirrids are boldly in view. Continue across the next field to reach another stile and then across the next field to a stile directly ahead.

Walk on with the fence on your left. Across the river you will now see the tower of Llanwenarth Church. The path now crosses the next field and heads towards a house close to the river. Go over a stile beside a gate and walk past the house to follow the edge of a field, keeping the fence on your right, towards another house. Then go up beside a stream in the direction of the Blorenge. The old farmhouse on the right is called 'Boat Farm' and it is obviously named after the old ferry crossing which used to be below this point.

Continue through the next two fields and pass beneath three sets of overhead cables. Go through a gate to the left of the last pylon and pass beneath the Heads of the Valleys Road, now following a concrete road which strangely peters out in the middle of a field. Continue across the field to reach a gate. Turn left along a pavement beside the Govilon road.

By a cottage on the left (Old Unicorn's Rest 1670), cross the road and climb over a large stone slab stile. Head up a field with a hedge on your left. Ascend a few stone steps and go over another slab stile. Keep straight on beside a fence to cross an old tram road (constructed by Crawshay Bailey) and go over a stile. Ascend a short flight of steps made of old railway sleepers. On reaching the old railway line, turn left and follow it to a bridge spanning the Blaenafon road. Descend some steps on the right. Then follow a gravel track steeply up to the canal.

Follow the canal towpath back to Llanfoist Wharf.

Llanfoist Wharf before Hill's Warehouse was converted into a dwelling.   *Chris Barber*

Opposite Hill's Warehouse, go down a flight of steps on the left and then walk down the lane past Llanfoist Church. Go across the main road and then head down the lane on the other side, to pass the Market Garden and then up and under the Heads of the Valleys Road. Turn a corner and you have now rejoined your outward route. Retrace your steps back to the start.

SKIRRID FAWR - 'The Holy Mountain'

'On fair clear days one could see the pointed summit of the Holy Mountain by Abergavenny. It would shine, I remember, a pure blue in the far sunshine; it was a mountain peak in a fairy tale.'

Arthur Machen, 'Far off Things'

Skirrid Fawr — 'The Holy Mountain'.   Chris Barber

These descriptive words of Arthur Machen bring back special memories to me. When I was a child, my family lived in a house just off Christchurch Road, on the edge of Newport and my father, a keen photographer had a special way of identifying days when visibility was particularly good. He would come into my bedroom first thing on a weekend morning and gaze intently out of the window in the direction of Caerleon-upon-Usk. If it was really clear and he could make out the bold but distant outline of Skirrid Fawr on the horizon, he would turn to me and say, "Yes it should be a good day for photographs, so we will head for the Black Mountains."

Skirrid sighting became infectious and I soon adopted the habit of looking through the window every morning to see if the grey smudge of this distant peak was visible. Then one fine day, when I had reached the grand old age of 6, my father announced that we were going to drive to Abergavenny and climb the Skirrid. So later that afternoon I climbed my first mountain (Well, to me it was a mountain), and touched my first trig' point. The day was made even more memorable because a gust of wind snatched my school cap and blew it away beyond retrieval.

Standing on the summit I stared in wonder across the valley and my father pointed out the Sugar Loaf and the Black Mountains. We turned around to face the opposite direction, gazed at the Graig and searched for the towers of White Castle perched on a low hill above Llanvetherine. Yes, the Skirrid will always have special memories for me and I walk to its summit several times every year to enjoy the ever-changing views.

It is not only the view from the summit that is constantly changing but the Skirrid itself. When seen from different angles it takes on a wide range of appearances. Sometimes it is a long ridge,or a mere hump. At other times it appears black and sinister with that wierd gash silhouetted against the sky.

People often ask me why it is called Skirrid Fawr. Well, the true Welsh name is of course Ysgyryd derived from Ysgur — to divide and Ysgyryd means separated. This is a reference to the lump on its western side which has slipped away from the summit giving it such a distinctive appearance. Another translation of the name suggests that it is a hill that has shivered or been shaken. Yet another explanation is that Ysgyryd is a shortened version of Ysgredig, meaning split. However it is also of interest to consider that the name is a corruption of 'cysegredig' which translates as sacred or holy. After all it is also known as the 'The Holy Mountain'.

Throughout the ages this isolated hill has held the respect of men — locals and travellers alike. Undoubtedly this awe must be attributed to the unusual shape of the peak and the various tales and legends that have been linked with it. My favourite one is that the great cleft on its north-west side was made when Noah's Ark glided over the side of the Skirrid during the Great Flood!

An alternative tradition is that the slip occurred at the time of the Crucifixion of Christ, when the hill 'was rent asunder by an earthquake and a bolt of lightning; and for this reason it is known as the Holy Mountain.'

Geologists, of course have a more logical but prosaic explanation for the origin of the great cleft. They say that it is a landslip caused largely to the inclination of the strata and the beds of intervening clay, but most people find the legends much more interesting.

Fred Hando climbed Skirrid Fawr with his young son Robert on Good Friday in 1953 and later described their ascent as follows:-

'It was a brilliant, breezy, blue day — a day for the mountains. The easy way to the Skirrid is from the Ross road. This route has many advantages in addition to its gradualness but it presents no challenge if the climber is over six and under eighty so we chose the northern approach.

'Between Llwyn Frank Farm and Pen-y-Parc, we came to a snow white cottage with two snow white cats sunning themselves on the window sill. "May we take this way to the Skirrid?" I asked the lady of the cottage. "You may," she replied, "but I don't envy you." Her voice was pretty and melodious, but under the rising intonation was a suggestion of sympathy.

'We climbed the stone steps and the stile to the open field. The Skirrid towered ahead. Did I mention a challenge? Matterhorn memories — for I had seen the Matterhorn at a distance — seemed perhaps an over-statement of the job ahead of us: the gradient of the eastern slope appeared to be only slightly less than the precipice on the right.

'After some exploration we found the winding "pony path". My companion, intolerant of my speed, went ahead at what seemed a supersonic velocity and was soon out of sight, while I enjoyed the rhythm of a few steps, and a view, a few steps and a view.

'A shout from above announced that one of us had reached the summit. I toiled upwards. The hours passed. Then with a gasp of relief, I flung myself into Jack o' Kent's heel-print — for you should know that the hollow in the top of the Skirrid which marks the site of the Llanfihangel (St. Michael's Church) was formed when Jack o' Kent leaped the four miles from the summit of the Sugar Loaf. Not satisfied with this and egged on by the contemptuos sniff of the Devil, Jack thereupon threw three enormous stones over twelve miles to Trellech, where they still remain.

'When Archdeacon Coxe climbed the Skirrid in 1800, he could see Hereford Cathedral. It has been one of my ambitions to see the Cathedral from the Skirrid and on this clear afternoon I had great hopes. Coxe wrote: "The spires of Hereford Cathedral gleam in the distant prospect," and he had not the benefit of my prismatic binoculars. But no cathedral spires or towers gleamed for us.

'Yet the views south over the familiar landmarks and the Channel, East where White Castle and all the little villages were crystal clear, North, where the Hereford hills threw their shadows on the Golden Valley, and West — ah! never have I seen the Black Mountains in such minute detail, with Pen-y-Fal and his big brothers in calm majesty and Cwmyoy like a giant carbuncle — such prospects dispelled my disappointment at missing the Hereford spires.

'After noting with satisfaction that the National Trust had taken over the mountain, we scrambled down through the heather while my companion gleefully experimented with his new double boomerang.'

Other writers have also compared the Skirrid with the mighty Swiss Matterhorn and perhaps there is a vague similarity in the appearance and the isolated situation of the two peaks, although in height there is an impressive difference of some 13,000 feet. Where mountains start and hills finish seems to be something of a mystery, for no official ruling seems to be laid down. Some mountaineers would argue that a true mountain is a 'Munro' — i.e. a summit over 3,000 feet. But others would claim that it is any summit over 2,000 feet. However, it is really perhaps purely a matter of personal opinion and the appearance of the peak in question.

The writer H. J. Massingham observes:-

'Among the mountains that adorn Abergavenny, like a portico of statues surrounding a memorial tablet or urn, it (Skirrid Fawr) speaks its own language. It is distinct from the oracular-looking Sugar Loaf, serene and aloof in the poise of its cone, classical in the symmetry of its balanced sides, as seen from the downlike curve of the Graig Serrethin far over the Little Skirrid in the crook of the Monnow away in northern Monmouthshire. It is a world apart from the grim and surly Blorenge which has no shape at all and no such language.'

ROUTE 16

THE TRADITIONAL WAY (2¾ miles, 2½ hours)

'The long spinal cord of the mountain rises steeply and smoothly for a whole mile hardly ever wider than thirty or forty feet and narrowing to ten or twelve. Finally, it comes to an abrupt termination northwards in a kind of notch or hook in the skyline which the up-reared back gives it its singular character.'

H.J. Massingham

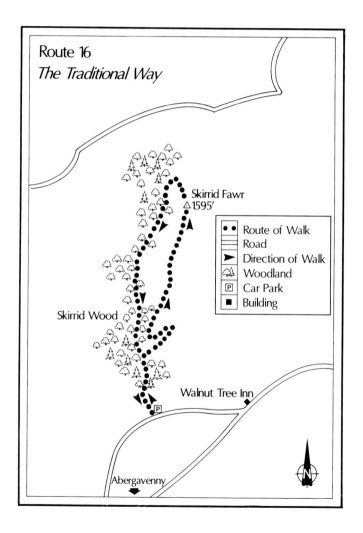

Start at a layby on the B4521 about three miles north-east of Abergavenny (SO 329164). Go over a stile near the edge of the layby and follow a path to reach a gate below a wood. From here a well- trodden path takes you up a series of steps through Skirrid Wood.

On reaching the top of the wood, go over a stile and turn right to pass through a picturesque dingle. Soon the path brings you onto the open hillside and up to the start of a narrow ridge about 1 mile in length, which gently rises towards the summit.

The views now open up on both sides and on a clear day they can be very satisfying with the slumbering mass of the Sugar Loaf and the Black Mountains on the left contrasting with open rolling farmland on the east side of the ridge. In due course the trig' point will be seen in the distance marking the summit.

A short distance before the summit is a large chunk of rock with an assortment of initials and names carved on it. It is referred to in one old guide book as *'a great stone shaped like a house called Cist Arthur . . . in English Arthur's Chest.'*

The summit is ringed by the oval fortification ditch of an Iron Age fort that does not appear to have been completed. It is most noticeable on the north side of the summit, particularly as seen from a distance when sunlight picks out the line of the low simple rampart.

Site of St. Michael's Chapel.   *Chris Barber*

Just in front of the trig' point two upright stones and a depression in the ground mark the site of St. Michael's Chapel.

The stones are about 2 feet high with chamfered edges are all that remain of the doorway to the chapel.

In 1680 John Arnold of Llanfihangel Court stated that he had seen, *'a hundred papists meet on the top of this hill called St. Michael's Mount where there is frequent meetings, and, eight or ten times in the year, sometimes sermons are preached there.'* It is significant that in Llanfihangel Court there is an oil painting dated 1680 that clearly shows the chapel standing on the summit of the Skirrid.

Old painting in Llanfihangel Court.   Chris Barber

Confirmation of Arnold's account was also given by John Scudamore of Kentchurch Court who claimed to *'have seen very great numbers of people on the top where there is a ruinous chapell and a stone with crosses on it, which was probably an altar. People with beads in their hands were kneeling towards the said stone.'*

J.T. Barber in 1807 wrote: *'There was formerly at the top of the Skyrrid a Roman Catholic Chapel dedicated to St. Michael of which no vestiges remain; but a remembrance of the site is preserved in a hollow place, formed by the superstitous, who resorting here on Michaelmas eve, carry away the earth to strew over the sepulchres of their friends.'*

Joseph Bradney, the Monmouthshire historian writing in 1906, commented: *'There is no account of the history of the chapel. It must be of great antiquity for, in the centre of the chapel, three parishes meet.'* These are the parishes of Llanddewi Skirrid, Llanfihangel Crucorney and Llantilio Pertholey.

In 1939 Skirrid Fawr was presented to the National Trust by Major Herbert and the N.T. emblem appears on the trig' point.

One may complete a circular route by descending to the foot of the northern slope. Experienced walkers who are used to very steep descents often use the direct route which goes down to the left. If you prefer a gentler route then either retrace your steps down the ridge or return along the ridge for about 50 yards and take a path leading down diagonally on the left, This will also bring you down to the foot of the north slope and a track can then be followed around to the left to pass below the cliffs of the north face and through the bottom of the 'landslip valley.' Years ago farmers used to dig large quantities of soil from this ravine and take it home by the sackful to sprinkle on their land to ensure a good harvest and keep the evil spirits away. The sacred soil was also sprinked on coffins at funerals and some country folk even managed to coonvince themselves that it came from the Holy Land. However the most popular belief was that St. Patrick had brought it from Ireland and that consequently no vermin or disease could exist on it.

This path leads pleasantly through the valley. A word of warning though, in summer it passes through high bracken which after a shower of rain will soak you with water.

On the hillside above you may notice a curious toadstool-shaped rock known as 'The Devil's Table'. It was here that his Satanic Majesty sat having tea when Jack o' Kent leaped across the valley from the Sugar Loaf to leave his huge heel-print on the side of the Skirrid.

Continue through the valley and then ascend slightly through the woods on the other side of the hill, where a path leads you around to rejoin your outward route.

AN EARLY ASCENT OF THE SKIRRID

William Coxe during his historic tour of the county in 1799 wrote a very dramatic description of his ascent to the summit of Skirrid Fawr. It is the earliest known documented account of such an excursion on this hill.

'After taking some refreshment and repose, I departed at two for the summit of the Skyrrid, on horseback, and accompanied by the same guide who had conducted me to the top of the Sugar Loaf. Having rode two miles along the road leading to White Castle, we attempted to ascend towards the south-western part of the mountain, which is distinguished with three small fissures. I soon discovered that the guide was unacquainted with the way, and on enquiring of a farmer, was informed that the usual route led by Landdewi Skyrrid; by his direction, however, we continued at the foot of the mountain, through fields of corn and pasture, and then proceeded along a narrow path, overspread with high broom, which in many places quite covered my horse. Forcing our way with some difficulty through this heathy wood, we rode over a moor, by the side of the stone wall and hedge which stretch at the base, reached the path leading from Landewi Skyrrid, and ascended on foot the grassy slope of the mountain.

'The heat was so intense, the fatigue I had undergone in the day so considerable, and the effort I impatiently made to reach the summit so violent that when I looked down from the narrow and desolate ridge, the boundless expanse around and beneath, which suddenly burst upon my sight, overcame me. I felt a mixed sensation of animation and lassitude, horror and delight, such as I scarcely ever before experienced even in the Alps of Switzerland; my spirits almost failed, even curiosity was suspended,.and I threw myself exhausted on the ground. These sensations in-

111

creased during my continuance on the summit: I several times attempted to walk along the ridge, but my head became so giddy as I looked down the precipitous sides, and particularly towards the great fissure, that I could not remain standing.

'I seemed only safe when extended on the ground, and was not therefore in a condition to examine and describe the beauties of the view. However, I took out my pencil, and made a few hasty notes. The ridge of the Skyrrid seemed to be about a mile in length, extremely narrow, in general not more than thirty or forty feet broad, and in some places only ten or twelve; its craggy surface is partly covered with scant and russet herbage, and exhibits only a stunted thorn, which heightens the dreariness of its aspect. After remaining half an hour on the top, incapable of making any further observations, I descended, and went round the eastern side of the mountain, where it terminates in an abrupt precipice near the large fissure.

'I walked across the meadows, along a gradual descent, through fine groves of oaks and Spanish chestnuts, to Llanfihangel house, an old mansion belonging to the Earl of Oxford. It was the ancient seat of the Arnold family, and was sold in 1722 to auditor Harley, ancestor of the present Earl. It is now inhabited only by a farmer, and contains nothing but some old furniture, a few family pictures, and some good impressions of Hogarth's prints. The place is distinguished by avenues of Scots first, which are the largest and finest in England. From the grounds near the front of the house, the Skyrrid presents itself with peculiar effect, the fissure seems like an enormous chasm, separating two mountains, whose impending and craggy summits vie in height and ruggedness.

'It was near six o'clock, and I hastened to join a party returning from the ruins of Llanthony Abbey. I partook of an elegant collation, provided by my friend Mr. Greene, which was spread on the banks of the Honddy: the wine, 'Interiore, nota Falerni,' was cooled in the limpid and murmuring stream; the evening was placid and serene, and I forgot the fatigues of the day in convivial intercourse and social conversation.'

Skirrid Fawr silhouetted against the sky.   Chris Barber

ROUTE 17

THE HARD WAY (6¾ miles, 4 hours)

'At some dim period, the night of the Crucifixion, say the locals, and call it in consequence "The Holy Mountain", a great landslip clave its summit in half, leaving one side precipitous, so that approaching it from two directions at any rate, it shows the outline of a complete though ragged peak, rising high above the wooded foreground and slightly changing its rugged profile at every fresh bend of the road.'

A.G. Bradley

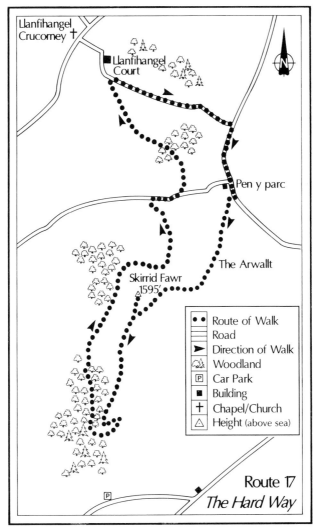

FRED HANDO . 1958
LLANFIHANGEL CRUCORNEY .

St. Michael's Church and Skirrid Fawr.   *Fred Hando*

This walk starts from the village of Llanfihangel Crucorney which is now by-passed by the A465 to Hereford. This means that the village no longer has to endure the constant stream of traffic which used to thunder past rocking the ancient foundations of the Skirrid Mountain Inn. Park in the roadside between the church and the inn.

The name Llanfihangel is derived from the word Llan meaning church and Angel which signifies Michael - the Archangel. Then we have the word Crucorney which is explained by the fact that the parish on the south side extends to the base of Skirrid Fawr, which results in the description Crug-y-Cornel, meaning 'Corner of the Rock', and this has been anglicized into Crucorney. Thus the name should really be Llanfihangel Crug y Cornel.

In Wales there are no less than 39 Llanfihangels and in Gwent alone there are 13 churches dedicated to St. Michael.

In the church porch is a stone on which is inscribed a memorial to James Hughes the village blacksmith who died in 1766:

'My Sledge and Hammer lies reclin'd
My Bellows too have lost his Wind
My Fire's extinct my Forge Decay'd
And in ye Dust my Vice is laid
My Coal is Spent my Iron is gone
My nails are Drove my Work is Done.'

114

When the church was being rebuilt in 1834, with money raised by public subscription, an ancient stone was revealed. On one side is a representation of the Virgin Mary with baby in her arms and on the reverse side is Christ on the cross between two thieves.

A survey carried out on the fabric of the church in 1974 revealed immense problems and it was decided that the nave roof was in a dangerous condition. So the Chancel was sealed off from the rest of the building and the congregation were then able to continue using this part of the church while the nave was re-roofed. However it was subsequently decided to restore only half of the Nave and leave the other part open to the sky as a *'garden of tranquility.'*

A marble stone commemorates William Morgan who died in 1827 after serving as curate and vicar here for no less than 59 years.

An eye-catching memorial is a beautiful sculptured head depicting Imogen Emily Hall. She was the daughter of the Hon. Sir W. Grove and she died in May 1866 at Llanfihangel Court, where she lived with her husband. Grief stricken, he commissioned Professor Romanelli of Florence to sculpture a fitting memorial. Also on the wall is a plaque commemorating Benjamin Matthews who lived at Pontrilas Court and was a founder member of the Alpine Club. In 1857 he made the first ascent of the Finsterhorn which was the highest peak in the Bernese Oberland Alps.

Behind the church you can look down into the valley to see the River Honddu which was diverted north-eastward after the Ice Age by a great moraine of glacial debris,now severed by a railway cutting.

Skirrid Mountain Inn.   *Chris Barber*

115

Further down the road is the Skirrid Mountain Inn. Its foundations probably date back to the 12th century and it is claimed to be the oldest pub in Wales and the second oldest in Britain. Originally it may have been built as a wayside halt for travelling monks.

At one time it served as a court house and Judge Jeffries, the famous hanging judge presided here on some occasions. No doubt he sentenced many a local man to death for committing offences that today would seem of little consequence. Marks on a beam above the well of the staircase were made by a rope used to hang the unfortunate wrongdoers, who were afterwards laid out on a stone slab 30 feet below. The last person to be executed here for sheep stealing was sentenced by Oliver Cromwell.

Alterations have been carried out to the pub in recent years, but at one time the ladies 'powder room,' used to be in the old condemned cell where prisoners who had been sentenced to death by hanging, spent their last miserable night. One of the ghosts seen there is said to be a one-eyed convict who cheated the hangman by stabbing himself to death.

The inn has a forbidding appearance with its grey stone, leaded windows and heavy iron-studed door, but inside it is cosy, atmospheric and a fascinating place to visit.

Having examined the village, go down a lane opposite the church, which takes you down to the A465. Cross with extreme care, for the traffic moves very fast along this stretch of road, and continue down the lane on the other side. It is, in fact, the drive to Llanfihangel Court. On reaching the court entrance follow the lane around to the right to shortly pass on the left a semi-derelict barn.

When the lane divides, keep straight on, ignore a footpath sign to the right and continue along the lane beside a stone wall. Pass through a gate and shortly look to the left to see a stone summer house in the grounds of the court. Further on you cross a stream and then continue along a rutted track leading through the trees. You will constantly be aware of the 'awesome outline' of the Skirrid glimpsed through the trees to the right.

Pass through a gate and the track soon starts gently ascending to shortly join a broader track. Keep straight on. Looking back now you will obtain a good view of Llanfihangel Court set in its parkland with Gaer Fawr rising to the left and the summit of Pen y Gadair Fawr in the distance on the right.

This fine old house set in a wooded valley was built in Tudor times and it has been the home of many diferent families during the last 400 years. Both Queen Elizabeth and Charles I are supposed to have stayed here and the coat of arms of the latter is displayed in the drawing room. It bears the date 1594 and a motto in Welsh 'Kofia dy Ddechre' which translates 'Remember thy origin.'

It is haunted by a mysterious white lady who is said to appear on the stroke of midnight. She glides down the terrace outside the mansion and passes along the great avenue of Scots Pines stretching towards the Skirrid and utters a piercing scream.

Shortly, turn right off the main track to cross a stream and go over a stile. Turn left and follow a fence to reach another stile. There is a good view now looking back towards the Sugar Loaf. Carry on beside the fence by the side of a rocky gully and after about 100 yards go over a stile on the left, opposite a der-

Northern approach to Skirrid Fawr.   Chris Barber

elict cottage. Continue up a sometimes muddy track, down which a stream may be flowing. This is an ancient hollow way with holly trees overhanging on either side.

At the time of writing the path is cluttered in places with fallen branches. Shortly, escape into the field on the left and head up to a stile beside a gate. On reaching a road, turn right and walk towards the prominent hump of Skirrid Fawr. Good views may be enjoyed from this road, taking in the Skirrid, Sugar Loaf, Bryn Arw, Gaer fort, Pen y Gadair Fawr and the Hatterrall ridge of the Black Mountains. On the other side of the road can be seen Garway Hill, Graig Syffrydin, Kymin Hill and the Trellech ridge.

On reaching a road junction, keep straight on, and after about 200 yards, follow a track to the right to pass through a gate. (If locked, remember to climb over on the hinged end). Continue up the slope beside a fenced gully which is an old hollow way. Look directly left now to see the towers of White Castle perched on a hill-top.

The summit of the Skirrid has been lost from view for a while, but it now appears gently rising above the skyline of the sloping field. Keep on beside the fence and go through a gate to cross an area of land known as the Arawllt.

Continue through the next two fields and make for a stile in the top fence. Now head straight up for about 50 yards and then bear slightly left to pass a couple of trees. Shortly you will join a broader track which diagonally ascends the northern slope of the Skirrid. To the left can be seen Llanddewi Church and the ajoining court of the same name.

117

You are now following an ancient ascent route which provided a direct way up to St. Michael's Chapel and was probably used by the pilgrims who struggled up this hillside several centuries ago, They came in large numbers on Good Friday andSeptember 29th, which is St. Michael's Day. This track is not as steep as the direct northerly ascent route further around to the right and soon the angle relents slightly bringing you up to the ridge at a point about 200 yards south of the summit. Go right and follow the ridge up to the summit.

'I found the wind so furious and irresistible on this enormous cone that I sensibly hurried forward in ascending; and such was the danger of standing on the narrow ridge that I dared not venture near it, for fear of being blown down the opposite side. The circulation of air is so rapid that it actually whistles in the grass.'

J.P. Malcolm 1805

In March 1972 the young people of St. Teilo's Church Llantilio Pertholey obtained permission from the National Trust to erect a 15 feet high wooden cross on this summit. The event took place on Good Friday and the youth of all dominations in Abergavenny were invited to participate in the procession and service. They left St. Teilo's Church at 3.15 p.m. carrying a large cross weighing 60 lbs. Between 80 and 90 teenagers took turns to carry it to the summit, where it was duly erected and an inter-denominational service was held.

Perhaps they had in mind the words of the mountaineer Frank Smythe, who once wrote: 'To climb a mountain is to tread not only the heights of earth, it is to adventure to the very boundaries of heaven.'

Having taken your fill of the view either return by the same route or for a longer walk descend the spine ridge of the Skirrid and at the end of the ridge descend to the left, following the traditional route. On reaching a stile on the left where the path leads down through the woods, ignore this turning and carry on beside the stone wall to make your way around the southern end of the hill. The path then continues through the trees and bracken along the lower slopes of the hill.

Believe it or not, a few years ago a walker managed to get thoroughly lost on the Skirrid. His story was subsequently reported in the local paper and it made amusing reading. He strayed off the path on the lower slopes and wandered deep into the woods. According to the newspaper report he claimed to be an *'experienced walker'*, but surely his experience must have been very limited for him to have got into difficulties in such a small wood. However he was well prepared for such an eventuality, for he was carrying a CB radio and put out a distress call. This was quickly picked up by an enthusiast and the information passed on to the police.

In due course the intrepid explorer managed to escape from the clutches of Skirrid Wood and made his way down to Skirrid Farm where he was met by a policeman who had spent four hours searching for him!

Ahead of you will be seen the famous Skirrid 'notch' through which the path passes, threading its way between boulders and slabs of rock. This 'landslide valley' was described by Archdeacon Coxe, as a *'stupendous fissure.'* On the other side of it the path leads you around to the base of the north face.

A variation on the legendary origin of this gash in the side of the Skirrid concerns another tale about the Dvil. One day he was testing his strength by throwing stones and from the top of the mountain he threw three great stones (they were thrown by Jack of Kent in other versions of the tale) towards the Wye Valley. They all fell close to each other at Trellech above Tintern, but as he went to cast a fourth one over to the distant hillside, his foot slipped and formed a deep hollow in the mountain. This caused him to lose his balance, and the last stone fell short of its mark.

John White described the prominent shape of Skirrid Fawr as follows:

'From a distance it presents a strange and wild appearance, which is rendered the more striking by the immense fissure in the mountain's side, splitting it, as it were, into two parts. What has been the cause of this has been an inquiry frequently made; and various are the suppositions laid down. There is of course, a legend which declares that it occurred at the time of the Crucifixion of Our Saviour, when the 'rocks were rent'. Others thought that this strange phenomenon was occasioned by numerous springs undermining the foundation. Various opinions have been advanced, but, we think, do not satisfactorily account for the phenomenon. If the mountain be closely examined, it will be found that its surface is covered with small slips, which could not have been produced by either of the causes mentioned. It appears to us that the slip arose from a long continued descent of rain, disturbing the particles of a loose sandy nature, of which this portion of the mountain is composed and thus causing the side to fall off the main body. Such cases are by no means unfrequent amongst the mountains around; but the most striking instance is that of the Darren, in the Vale of Ewyas.'

On reaching two gates side by side, with a fence in between, go through the right hand one and head down beside a gully to reach a stile. Bear left on the other side and then walk down beside a fence adjacent to the gully. At the end of the field go left over a stile, and across a gully to reach a gate by a barn. Continue to another stile, head down to a gate and turn right along a road at Llwyn Franc. This name means Frank's Grove and the house of this name belonged in the 17th century to Charles Morgan of Llantilio Pertholey.

After about ¼ mile go over a stile on the left beside a gate. Head down to the bottom of a field and go through a gap in a hedge. Continue through the next field to cross a stile in a fence.

Keep straight on down through the next field and then bear left slightly to go over a double stile in a fence and then continue straight on through a wood. Cross a little footbridge spanning a rock-strewn gully and go over a stile. Head straight across the next field to pass left of a small clump of trees. Now join a track leading on beside a fence. Go through a gate and head towards a corrugated-iron barn, keeping the fence on your right. Go through another gate and rejoin your outward route which will lead you past the outer wall of Llanfihangel Court.

NINE HUNDRED YEARS IN THE HISTORY OF ABERGAVENNY

1090: Hamelyn de Balun, first Lord of Abergavenny, dies.

1093c: Abergavenny town wall is constructed.

1094: William Rufus the son of William the Conqueror (who died in 1087) pays a visit to Abergavenny whilst on his way to subdue a rebellion of the men of Gwent, Brecknock and the Gower peninsula.

1135: Richard de Clare is murdered by the Welsh.

1165: Walter Earl of Hereford and 3rd Lord of Abergavenny, is appointed Constable of England and the Lordship of Abergavenny is transfered to his brother Henry.

1172: Abergavenny Castle is attacked and captured by the Welsh and Henry is killed. The castle remains in the possession of Sitsyllyt ap Dfynwal until 1176, when it is restored to Willian de Braose, who succeeds his uncle Henry as the fifth Lord of Abergavenny.

1175: Sitsyllt surrenders the castle and it is returned to the Norman lordship.

1177: Christmas Day massacre at Abergavenny Castle.

1182: Abergavenny Castle is attacked and partially destroyed by the Welsh.

1188: Archbishop Baldwyn and Giraldus Cambrensis visit Abergavenny to preach the third Crusade.

1191: William de Braose gives King Richard 1,000 marks to have the wardship of Gilbert, Lord of Monmouth.

1206: William de Braose petitions King John for the possession of Grosmont, Skenfrith and Whitecastle and and offers to pay 800 marks, 3 horses, 5 hunters and 25 hounds.

1209: Estates of William de Braose are confiscated by King John.

1211: King John visits Abergavenny and takes Maud de Braose and her son William to Windsor Castle where they are imprisoned and starved to death.

1213: William de Braose dies in France. Giles de Braose becomes sixth Lord of Abergavenny.

1215: Giles dies at Gloucester and is buried in the choir of of Hereford Cathedral. His title is taken by his third son Reginald who becomes the seventh Lord of Abergavenny. Abergavenny Castle is placed in the hands of a Royal Constable.

1222: Reginald dies and his son William becomes the eighth Lord. He has an intrigue with Prince Llewellyn's wife — Joan.

1230: He is found out and hanged. Having no sons his four daughters become co-heiresses. Isobel the eldest daughter married David the son of Prince Llewellyn. Eva the third daughter married William de Cantelupe and she received the Lordship and the Abergavenny estates. She conferred the Lordship of Abergavenny to her husband who became the ninth Lord.

1233: King Henry III visits Abergavenny.

1256: William de Cantelupe dies. His son George is only two years of age, but he becomes the 10th Lord.

1257: Eva Cantelupe dies and is buried in St. Mary's Church, Abergavenny. Her tomb is in the Herbert Chapel.

1262: The Welsh under Llewellyn ap Gruffyd attack Abergavenny Castle.

1273: George de Cantelupe, tenth lord of Abergavenny dies.

1291: Edward I holds a council at Abergavenny Castle lasting three weeks.

1319: John de Hastings, Lord of Abergavenny, petitions Pope John XXII to reform the priory.

1341: Black Death hits Abergavenny and many people die.

1348: Lawrence Hastings falls a victim of the Black Death and is the last Lord of Abergavenny to be buried in St. Mary's Priory Church.

1349: Black Death hits Abergavenny with a vengeance. One fifth of the population die.

1389: The last Lord of Abergavenny is killed whilst jousting at the castle.

1402: People of Abergavenny riot against the castle.

1408: Owain Glyndwr sets fire to the town.

1450: Sir Edward Nevill becomes the first baron of Abergavenny to enter Parliament.

1495-1507: Jasper Tudor, Earl of Pembroke holds the Lordship of Abergavenny.

1536: Dissolution of the Monasteries. Only thirteen monks are left at St. Mary's Priory.

1538: John Leland the Antiquarian pays a visit to Abergavenny.

1542: King Henry VIII Grammar School is founded in St. John's Church. Abergavenny is granted a Royal Charter by Henry VIII.

1543: St. Mary's Priory is dissolved.

1602: A new Market Hall is erected. (It stood in the road between the present Boots and the Town Hall).

1638: Charles I grants a Royal Charter to Abergavenny.

1645: Abergavenny Castle is made uninhabitable on the orders Charles I.

1657: Oliver Cromwell grants Abergavenny a Royal Charter.

1689: Abergavenny Royal Charter is confiscated by William III.

1739: John Wesley preaches in Abergavenny.

1784: George Nevill the fifteenth lord of this line is created Viscount Nevill and Earl of Abergavenny.

1794: New Market Hall designed by John Nash is built at a cost of £810.

1795: South Gate is demolished.

1796: Street lighting comes to Abergavenny. Twenty oil lamps are 'ordered to be put in proper places in the town'.

1813: French prisoners are incarcerated in Abergavenny after Napoleon's defeat. Some 80 officers and about 200 soldiers and sailors are brought here. The rank and file are lodged in rooms in the castle and also in some large barns in the immediate district. The officers being on parole are billetted in private houses in different parts of the town. They are not allowed to go further than one mile from their place of residence, under risk of being re-captured and sent to prison.

1814: Llanfihangel tramroad is completed.

1815: Cannons are hauled onto the castle keep mound and fired to celebrate the defeat of Napoleon at the battle of Waterloo.

1818: Victorian sham castle keep is built by the Marquis of Abergavenny.

1823: Abergavenny Gas Works is constructed by Thomas Davies and he is allowed to lay gas mains through the town in return for supplying 20 gas lamps free of charge.

1834: Abergavenny Cricket Club is formed.

1840: Holy Trinity Church is built.

1844: First Abergavenny Horse Show is held. (It is now called the Abergavenny and Borders Agricultural Show).

1848: Eisteddfod held in Abergavenny under the patronage of the Prince of Wales.

1851: Joint Counties Lunatic Asylum is opened at Pen-y-Fal.

1854: Abergavenny & Hereford Railway is opened and the first train to arrive in Abergavenny clanks its way down 'the bank' from Llanfihangel and comes to a squeaky stop at the new Abergavenny Station.

1863: Abergavenny Cattle Market is built.

1864: Edwin Morgan launches the 'Abergavenny Gazette', a 1½d weekly paper, from his home in 21 Nevill Street. It only survives for a few issues.

1865: Castle Street Girls School is opened on ground formerly occupied as a sheep market.

1871: First edition of Abergavenny Chronicle is published on August 12th by Edwin Morgan at a premises in Frogmore Street. Abergavenny Town Hall is constructed.

1879: On August 17th, a cat in Abergavenny gives birth to four kittens, three of which have six toes on each pad, the fourth having five toes on each fore pad and four toes on the hind pads. All the toes on the pads are similar to those of ordinary cats. The Improvement Commissioners decide to extend the limits of the town to about eight times its existing area.

1880: Brecon & Abergavenny Canal is taken over by the Great Western Railway Company.

1881: Marquis of Abergavenny leases the Castle grounds to the Abergavenny Improvements Commission.

1882: West front of St. Mary's Church rebuilt.

1883: Bailey Park is opened. Cymdeithas Cymmreigyddion y Fenni is established in Abergavenny to encourage Welsh culture.

1891: Coldbrook Estate is purchased by Lady Llanover.

1892: Abergavenny Golf Club is established.

1894: Abergavenny becomes an urban district.

1898: Formal opening of Abergavenny Grammar School and Girls Intermediate School in Pen-y-Pound. This 'is said to be the most important event that has occurred in Abergavenny during the last 30 years.'

1899: Queen Victoria grants a Charter of Incorporation, making the town a municipal borough governed by a mayor, four aldermen and eleven councillors. The first Mayor to be appointed for Abergavenny is Joseph Bishop.

1900: Abergavenny Thursdays Football Club is founded from among local shop assistants.

1905: Foundation stone of the Abergavenny Carnegie Library is laid — with Abergavenny incorrectly spelt with three N's!!

1913: Welsh National Eisteddfod held at Abergavenny in the Castle grounds. General Sir Baden-Powell, Chief Scout paid a visit to Abergavenny on Easter Monday afternoon.

Broncho Bill's great Wild West Exhibition together with a large two-ring circus visits the Fair Field on Thursday March 20th for one day only. 'The greatest spectacle of all is the attack on the Deadwood Coach. It is carried out on a huge scale and no less than 150 horses, cowboys and Indians take part.'

1914: A public meeting is held in the Market Hall to encourage recruits for what is known as Lord Kitchener's Army. The spacious hall is very crowded and the proceedings are marked by tremendous enthusiasm. Mr. and Mrs. Curre offer Maindiff Court to the British Red Cross Society as a Convalescent Home. The canal bursts its banks above Skew Bridge, near Llanfoist when about 30 feet of bank gives way, 'weakened it is thought by the burrowing of moles'.

1915: Marquis of Abergavenny dies and estates are sold off with the exception of the castle grounds.

1919: Nevill Hall is sold to the Board of Management of the Blaina and District Hospital.

1920: A Crucifix is erected in the grounds of the Catholic Church in Penypound as a war memorial to the fallen members of that church. The bronzed figure is a life-sized representation of Christ and is mounted on a cross of old oak with a porched roof. The unveiling ceremony is performed on Good Friday.

1921: Alderman J.R. Beckwith is elected as Mayor of Abergavenny. He is able to claim the distinction of being the first working-man in the town to be awarded this honour, following ten years continuous service on the Town Council.

1922: The War Memorial at the Town Hall is unveiled by the Lord Lieutenant of Monmouthshire. The Town Council discusses the question of installing electricity in the town and appoints a committe to consider the matter.

1923: A new fire engine is purchased by Abergavenny Rural District Council. People living in the rural district can now rest content that should a fire unfortunately break out on their premises, there is available the most modern and efficient appliance for dealing with it properly.

1924: A new bowling green in Bailey Park is officially opened by Major Jacob, the Mayor. Bailey Park Bowling Club is officially formed.

1925: Mr. Tom Williams of Monk Street dies. He was a native of Abergavenny and 70 years of age. For 45 years he had been in business in the town, as a carpenter and joiner, but he was best remembered as the last man to ring the curfew bell at St. John's Church.

1926: A War Memorial tablet is unveiled at St. Mary's Church and dedicated to the memory of the men from St. Mary's who gave their lives in the Great War.

1929: Andre Robe Mcwhyte, a Newfoundler of Scots parentage whilst walking around the world to win a 40,000 dollar wager, passes through Abergavenny on September 14th, after covering 8,300 miles in a little over two years. His log book is signed by Colonel J.G. Bishop, Mayor of Abergavenny. It is his intention to finish the walk in 1934.

1931: Llwyn Du reservoir is covered. The introduction of electricity to the town is discussed at a meeting of Abergavenny Chamber of Trade. A fierce storm hits Abergavenny. 'Ruin and desolation was everywhere and none of the residents of Mill Street will ever forget their terrifying experiences. Monmouth Road was flooded to a depth of eight feet.'

1932: Duke and Duchess of York (later to be King George V and Queen Mary) visit Abergavenny on 17th March.

1933: Last commercial traffic to pay a toll on the Brecon & Abergavenny Canal.
1934: Abergavenny Cricket Club celebrate their centenerary. Empire Day is celebrated and the Abergavenny Branch of the Womens' Unionist Association entertain 400 children to tea in the Town Hall. An Air Display is held at Llanfoist Farm to raise funds for the Victoria Cottage Hospital and stimulate a wider and greater interest in British civil aviation.

1935: The Sugar Loaf is given to the National Trust by Viscountess Rhondda.

1936: An air display is organised by the British Empire Display at Llanfoist Farm.

1939: An open air swimming pool is built in Bailey Park. The summit of Skirrid Fawr, consisting of 169 acres of wooded hillside is presented to the National Trust by Major J. Herbert.

1941: A proposal to relieve congestion in the main streets of Abergavenny by the adoption of a one-way traffic scheme is put before the monthly meeting of the Town Council.

1942: Rudolph Hess is taken from the Tower of London (last man to be held there) and brought to Abergavenny where he is interred in Maindiff Court Hospital. Here he is confined until the end of the war in 1945.

1943: A 'Wings for Victory Week' is staged in Abergavenny with the aim of raising £100,000 towards the purchase of two Sunderland Flying Boats. The local Home Guard hold a mock 'battle of Abergavenny'. 'A' and 'C' Companies have the task of defending the town against an invading force of 'airbourne enemy troops' represented by the Sector Reserve.

1944: The Abergavenny and District War Savings Committe have since 1940, now contributed £1,604,000 in savings to the National Treasury.

1945: V.E. day is celebrated in Abergavenny. Street parties, races, dancing, community singing and fun of all kinds are enjoyed by the jubilant inhabitants. At one party an effigy of Hitler was hung and then burnt. A prize was offered to the person who was able to accurately guess the number of nails in 'Adolf's' size 10 boots!

1950: Princess Margaret visits Abergavenny during a tour of South Wales. She inspects Coed Glas Nursery and takes a keen interest in the 23 infants there. Then she goes on to Cefn Tila Court, near Usk, to have lunch with Lord Raglan.

1951: Lightning causes damage to Castle House, splits a few chimneys and puts the town's telephones out of order on Wednesday 2nd May. Abergavenny Town Council approve a recommendation that £1,200 should be spent on ornamental gates for the Swan Meadow as part of the town's contribution to the Festival of Britain. A new telephone exchange which can cater for 1,100 subscribers is opened in Frogmore Street.

1952: Priory House is demolished.

1953: Nevill Hall Hospital is opened in January to serve North Monmouthshire. Coldbrook House is demolished. The Cattle Market is improved with the construction of a covered sale ring and better penning accomodation in the attested hed section is provided. The total cost is more than £4,000.

1954: The Seven Hills of Abergavenny race is held.

1956: Having served the community for over 100 years, Tabernacle Methodist Church, Victoria Street closes. It amalgamates with Castle Street Methodist Church.

1957: Slum clearance of Flannel Street and Tudor Street commences.

1958: Last train from Abergavenny to Merthyr runs on Sunday 5th January. A £26,000 major improvement scheme is carried out at the Cattle Market with a new sale ring, offices and a lorry wash provided.

1959: In July of this year Abergavenny Museum is opened by Lord Raglan. It is located in the house adjoining the castle keep and has 100 exhibits on display.

1960: Grave yard on north side of St. Mary's Priory Church is converted into a Garden of Rest.

1962: In August, the first stage of the Heads of the Valleys Road from the Hardwick Roundabout is opened at a cost of £700,000.

1963: First Three Peaks Trial is held on Saturday 9th March. Queen Elizabeth II and the Duke of Edinburgh visit Abergavenny on 10th May. The Beatles play at Abergavenny Town Hall on 22nd June.

1964: During the excavation of foundations for the new Post Office, evidence of the Roman fort of Gobannium comes to light. 700 people attend St. Mary's Priory Church to take part in the B.B.C. Television programme 'Songs of Praise'. Abergavenny Young Farmers hold their 21st anniversary dinner at the Town Hall. This is the first dinner to be held there with a licensed bar.

1965: Abergavenny Borough Council open Linda Vista Gardens to the public. Lt. Colonel H.M. Llewellyn of Llanfair Grange buries the hide of Foxhunter, a former champion show-jumper and Olympic gold medalist, on the top of Blorenge Mountain. A casket containing the hide is placed in a cavity in a natural outcrop overlooking four counties, and a plaque setting out Foxhunter's most memorable achievements is placed above it.

1966: The 18th century gateway to Old Court is demolished, being considered unsafe after the adjoining buildings were pulled down. The first traffic warden is appointed in Abergavenny. 'After a 4 hour training course at Headquarters, the warden, Mr. Horace Davies, is attached to Abergavenny police station in Baker Street.'

1967: Merthyr, Tredegar & Abergavenny Railway is closed. Abergavenny Soroptomist Society is formed.

1968: Abergavenny and District Civic Society is formed. Abergavenny is twinned with Oestringen in Germany and the Oestringen Association is formed to develop links between the two towns. The first Welsh Motor Show is held in Abergavenny Town Hall.

1969: The new Nevill Hall Hospital is opened.

1970: Saint David Lewis of Abergavenny is canonised.

1971: Abergavenny Market Hall is listed as an historic building. The Abergavenny Chronicle celebrates its centenary. Congratulations are sent by the Queen 'to all concerned with the publication of this newspaper on the attainment of its Centenerary and her best wishes to all its readers.' Abergavenny Museum is handed over to the borough council. The first decimal notice makes its appearance in Abergavenny when a board is put up in Castle Street car park listing the charges:- Cars 5p per Day and Cars with trailers 10p per Day. Previously the chargers were 1s and 2s.

1972: Abergavenny Borough Council approves a £150,000 scheme for the improvement of the Cattle Market. Lloyd's Bank achieve their centenerary for the local branch and hold a reception which is attended by their oldest customer, 104 year old Mrs Butt. She was also the oldest resident in Abergavenny and died 5 months later, just before her 105th birthday. The Town Hall Clock is also 100 years old. Sadly it suffers from periods of incorrect time-keeping due to being very sensisitve to temperature changes and also to the flock of pigeons which nest in its works.

1974: In August, Abergaveny has a mayor and town council once again and the new mayor is Councillor Pugsley an alderman on the former Abergavenny borough council. The change came after 4 months of being a community council.

1975: Brecon & Abergavenny Canal bursts its bank at Llanfoist. Abergavenny by-pass opens. the 3½ mile stretch of road from Hardwick roundabout to Lonely cottage was built at a cost of £2 million.

1976: Abergavenny experiences the longest spell of dry weather since records began. There is a spate of fires on the tinder dry hill-sides, with the worst fires in living memory on the Blorenge and Deri. First Annual Steam Rally is held in Bailey Park, organised by the Veteran and Vintage Abergavenny Association.

1977: The go-ahead is given for work to start on repairing 5 kilometers of the Monmouth and Brecon Canal at an estimated cost of £483,000. It is the largest project undertaken by the Manpower Services Commission in Wales.

1978: Abergavenny and District Tourist Association is formed to promote the town and district as a tourist area.

1979: The ancient Tithe Barn is turned into a saleroom for fine art and antiques. It is officially opened by the new Mayor of Abergavenny, Councillor Rosa Norris. The building has previously served as a theatre, a corn merchant's store, a discotheque and a computer work-shop.

1980: In January, Abergavenny suffers the worst floods in living memory.

1981: A 250 year old barn in Castle Street is demolished. Work begins on the first stage of the restoration of the keep at Abergavenny Castle.

1982: Scaffolding is removed from 'Red Square' when a new building is completed at the end of Flannel Street. An 'ambitious' plan to provide an arcade of shops in the middle of Abergavenny is considered by Monmouth District Council's Planning Committe.

1983: The Abergavenny Chronicle is sold by the Berrows Newspaper Group to Tindle Newspapers Ltd. An article on Abergavenny appears in the New York Times.

1986: Floodlighting is installed at Abergavenny at a cost of £1,200 raised by Abergavenny Local History Society.

1987: 200 former residents of Tudor Street attend a reunion party at the Castle Keep, hosted by singer Bryn Yemm who was also born in the street. The homes of these people were demolished in 1958. The stonework on the Town Hall is cleaned. An archaeological dig on a site adjacent to W.H. Smith in Cross Street reveals Roman artifacts dating back to 50 A.D.

1988: An Abergavenny time capsule, in stainless steel is buried in a wall at Tan House while it is being converted into retirement houses. It contains a copy of the Abergavenny Chronicle, a magistrates' court list, a King Henry VIII School magazine, credit cards, a set of minted coins, a set of stamps, a letter explaining the contents and a short history of the Tan House, with a map of 1804. These items were chosen to represent everyday life in Abergavenny. Six telephone boxes in Abergavenny are declared historic monuments to prevent them from being removed. Proposals to 'pedestrianise' Nevill Street and part of Frogmore Street are approved by Monmouth Borough Council. Five thousand and forty changes of the method 'Abergavenny Surprise Royal' are rung at St. Mary's Priory Church to celebrate the 40th Anniversary of the restoration of the bells. The peal lasted for 3 hours 17 minutes. Planning approval is given for the controversial Turkey Factory on a site near the Hardwick roundabout.

1990: Abergavenny celebrates its 900th anniversary of the founding of the town around the castle and priory in 1090.

ADDITIONAL INFORMATION

Sugar Loaf from Skirrid Fawr.   Chris Barber

THE THREE PEAKS TRIAL

The Three Peaks Trial has been organised as an endurance walk since March 1963. Originally it was designed for the walker of limited experience who was interested in testing his or her stamina and skill at map reading. It was felt that this route was ideal for such a purpose being very safe, with well established tracks and yet requiring careful map reading to ensure that the most suitable route was followed. Being a circular walk with Abergavenny in the centre, retirement from the event was no serious problem.

In the early days of The Three Peaks Trial it started from Crickhowell Youth Hostel (now defunct) and the majority of the entrants came for the weekend. A briefing was given on the Friday evening and the walk commenced at 8.00 a,m. the following morning, the object being to visit the summits of the three dominant peaks of Abergavenny: Blorenge, Skirrid Fawr and Sugar Loaf. The route from Crickhowell was approximately 22 miles in length and entrants were offered the choice of walking it in a clockwise or anti-clockwise direction. Certificates were presented to all entrants who completed the route successfuly.

The very first event was advertised in a YHA magazine and it attracted twenty entrants. It was to have taken place in February, but unfortunately severe snow conditions caused the event to be postponed. The six entrants who had managed to brave the elements and arrive at Crickhowell Youth Hostel were taken on a caving trip on Mynydd Llangattock, a limestone escarpment, above Crickhowell, instead. It was their first experience of this activity and they all enjoyed themselves so much that they were quite pleased that the walk had been postponed. One of the walkers had brought a pair of home made snow shoes to wear on the event, but to his disappointment they failed to survive their initial test on the journey to the cave through deep snow, falling to pieces after the first hundred yards!

A month later on Saturday 9th March, the first successful Three Peaks Trial was held. This time the weather was wet and windy. Twenty four people took part and they found conditions on the slopes of the Blorenge so uncomfortable with unceasing rain and a powerful wind that fourteen of them decided to call it a day on reaching Abergavenny. The remaining ten walkers, still close together, headed for Skirrid Fawr. By 2.30 p.m. nine of them had passed through the checkpoint on the summit, where the marshall had been trying to keep warm for two lonely hours. The tenth walker was accounted for later on, at 'The Crown' in Pant-y-Gelli! By now the rain had turned all the roads into watercourses, making it necessary, sometimes to take to the fields.

In the late afternoon the weather brightened considerably and all ten walkers reached the summit of the Sugar Loaf where they were served with hot coffee on a snow-covered ledge. From there they descended to Crickhowell and the first man home was Alistair Mackinnon who completed the twenty two mile route in about eight hours,

The event was enjoyed so much by those who took part that it was decided to make it an annual walk for the following three years at least. In 1964 it was advertised more widely and there were so many applicants that due to the limitations of accomodation at the Youth Hostel in Crickhowell (for initially it was a YHA members only event) it was decided to hold two separate events in March and October of that year. This twice a year programme was maintained for several years.

People of all ages, shapes and sizes came to tackle the walk and they were often accompanied by canine companions. Neville Tandy (well-known now as the organiser of the 'Reservoir Roundabout' and the 'Mid Wales Marathon') took his seven year old son on the walk one year and the plucky lad became the youngest person to complete the walk, much to the embarrassment of some of the retirements! Groups of Gwent Police Cadets and youngsters from Bodenham Manor School in Herefordshire regularly entered the event and it became a useful part of their training programme.

In 1975 a decision was made to transfer the starting point of the event to Abergavenny, where the Tredillion Scout Hut in the Fairfield Car park, near the centre of the town provided excellent facilities. By moving the start to Abergavenny the route was shortened by about five miles and the amount of road walking was pleasingly reduced. A few years later the Youth Hostel at Crickhowell closed, so a change of venue would have been necessary anyway.

The Three Peaks Trial is now a firmly established event on the walkers' calendar and it now attracts as many as two hundred entrants. It has been organised by the Cardiff local YHA Group for the last fifteen years and the name and adress of the current organiser may be obtained by contacting the YHA Office, 4th Floor, 1, Cathedral Road, Cardiff CF1 9HA.

LOCAL FACILITIES

Abergavenny Leisure Centre: Situated at King Henry VIII School, Old Hereford Road.

Bus Station: Near Swan Hotel, Cross Street.

Car Parks (free): Fairfield, Park Road. Market Street, behind Market Hall. Monmouth Road, beside Bus Staion (toilets). Priory Car Park, Monk Street (fee payable), Lion Street, Castle Street, near main Post Office (toilets). Castle Meadows, off Tudor Street.

Hill Residential College: Situated off Pen-y-Pound, adjacent to the King Henry VIII School.

Library: Baker Street, Abergavenny.

Museum: Abergavenny Castle Grounds.

Main Post Office: St. John's Square, Abergavenny.

Police Station: Gwent Constabulary, Tudor Street, Abergavenny.

Railway Station: Signposted off the Monmouth Road.

Theatres: Borough Theatre in the Town Hall and the Gwent Drama Theatre in Pen-y-Pound.

Tourist Information Centre: Bus Station.

Distances from Abergavenny: Hereford 24 miles, Newport 19 miles, Cardiff 32 miles, Brecon 32 miles, Brecon 21 miles. Bristol 40 miles, Birmingham 91 miles, London 143 miles, Shrewsbury 76 miles, Swansea 48 miles.

Market Days: Cattle Market, Tuesdays. General Market, Tuesdays and Fridays.

Early Closing Day: Thursday.

ACKNOWLEDGEMENTS

I am grateful to the *Abergavenny Chronicle* for allowing me to look through their back copies which contain some fascinating material. My thanks are also due to Wilf Davies and Anna Tucker for their helpful comments on the manuscript. Albert Lyons I thank for the loan of several photographs from his impressive collection, and Ken Flowers for details and pictures of his Seven Hills record achievements.

Sally Davies is thanked for her illustrations depicting the 'Massacre at Abergavenny Castle', and Michael Blackmore for his drawings previously published in my book *Cordell Country*. My gratitude is also extended to Mike Amos for his assistance with the maps, and Derek of Lawton Graphics for designing the cover.

Steve Lawless and David Tilton of Able TypeSetters are also thanked for their quick and efficient service, and Mid Wales Litho for their high quality printing.

OTHER TITLES BY CHRIS BARBER

Walks in the Brecon Beacons.

Exploring the Waterfall Country.

Ghosts of Wales.

Exploring the Brecon Beacons National Park.

Exploring Gwent.

Mysterious Wales.

More Mysterious Wales.

Cordell Country.

The Romance of the Welsh Mountains.

Hando's Gwent (Volume 1)

Hando's Gwent (Volume 2)

The Ancient Stones of Wales (Jointly with John G. Williams).